Little League®

DRILLS
AND
STRATEGIES

Ned McIntosh

CB

CONTEMPORARY BOOKS

Library of Congress Cataloging-in-Publication Data

McIntosh, Ned.
   Little league drills and strategies.

   1. Little League Baseball, Inc.   2. Baseball for children—
United States—Coaching.   3. Baseball for children—United
States—Training.   I. Title.
GV880.5.M338   1987   796.357'62   87-5258
ISBN 0-8092-4789-5

Photographs by Nicholas Photography and Mike Powers

Published by Contemporary Books
A division of NTC/Contemporary Publishing Group, Inc.
4255 West Touhy Avenue, Lincolnwood (Chicago), Illinois 60712-1975 U.S.A.
Copyright © 1987 by Ned McIntosh
All rights reserved. No part of this book may be reproduced, stored in a retrieval
system, or transmitted in any form or by any means, electronic, mechanical,
photocopying, recording, or otherwise, without the prior written permission of
NTC/Contemporary Publishing Group, Inc.
Printed in the United States of America
International Standard Book Number: 0-8092-4789-5
00 01 02 03 04 05 BH 32 31 30 29 28 27 26 25 24 23 22 21 20 19 18 17 16

Since I dedicated my first book, *Managing Little League Baseball,* to my three sons, it is only fitting that I dedicate this one to my wife Elaine and my daughters Bethann, Amy, and Lynne, who put up with an absentee husband/father every spring when they call "Play Ball!" at the local Little League field.

CONTENTS

INTRODUCTION

Upon the publication of *Managing Little League Baseball*, my first venture in writing a book, I was pleasantly surprised at the attention it evoked. Favorable reviews appeared in *USA Today*, the *Chicago Tribune*, and a host of other newspapers that picked up a review on the UPI wire service. I was even interviewed (via telephone) on a San Francisco radio talk show on sports. Apparently there *was* a need for a book on Little League, written by a father/coach for other parent/coaches.

Interestingly, the chapter that most reviewers chose to headline was the one on parents and pressure. The headline in the *Chicago Tribune* article was "Little League Primer Strikes at Adult Errors"; in the Huntsville, Alabama, *Times* it was "Little League Parents Strike Out!" And the interview on the San Francisco radio talk show centered on the subject of dealing with redneck parents. Unfortunately, five years after having written "Parents and Pressure," the problem has remained just as severe, and I have a few more things to say about it in this book.

Something I wasn't prepared for when my first Little League book was published was "fan mail." I received a number of letters, mostly from other coaches and managers. For the most part they wrote to say they shared my coaching philosophy of "keep it simple, make it fun." Some said they wished there had been more diagrams and pictures, illustrating the practice drills and strategies described. Some coaches said they wished I had covered particular subjects that were omitted; the two most requested subjects were pregame warmups and successful fund-raising campaigns.

In 20 years of Little League experience, I have never managed a team that had a losing season. Some managers (obviously of teams with losing seasons) asked for my formula for success. After thinking about that assignment, I finally decided that there *is* a formula that will guarantee a winning season. It is the same formula that the Little League Managers in Taiwan use with boys who, generally speaking, are not as big or strong as average American Little Leaguers; yet the All-Star team from Taiwan has dominated the Little League World Series over the years. My formula would be based on three elements that I dwell on in this book:

1. drilling the basics
2. promoting the practice philosophy of "keep it simple, make it fun"
3. practice, practice, practice!

I am happy also to share the coaching techniques that other coaches have shared with me. One coach in particular who wrote was Mike Powers, who manages his son's team in the Little League of St. Matthews, Kentucky, near Louisville. We have become pen/phone pals, corresponding and calling each other from time to time, comparing notes on how our respective teams are doing and sharing coaching tips and techniques. Mike is a strong advocate of my "keep it simple, make it fun" coaching philosophy, yet has enough different approaches that I have incorporated some of his drills and strategies with my own and with those suggested by other coaches, to give you a blend of ideas from different parent/ coaches from different parts of the country.

My business travels take me to many cities, and it is always a temptation when passing a book store to see if *Managing Little League Baseball* is on the shelves with the other books on sports. Frequently it is, and almost always it is the only available book on Little League baseball. There is no short-age of books on how to play adult baseball, but the Little League coach, who quickly realizes that there are more differences than similarities between adult and Little League baseball, still finds little help in libraries and bookstores. We hope that this book, in addition to *Managing Little League Baseball*, will give all the help needed for a successful experience in Little League.

Do you need to read both books to get the whole story of how to coach a Little League team? Not necessarily, since each stands pretty much on its own. *Managing Little League Baseball* gives an overview of the coaching philosophy of making the game of baseball simple and fun for young kids getting their first introduction to it. *Little League Drills and Strategies* expounds the same philosophy, but goes further to give a coach a guaranteed formula for a winning season, using easy-to-understand drills and strategies.

When I wrote *Managing Little League Baseball*, the youngest of my three sons was completing his last year in Little League, ready to move on to Senior League. I elected to stay as a Little League manager in order to give him the opportunity to make it on his own, without the benefit of, or disadvantage of, being the manager's son. He proved to both of us that he could do it, and he has gone on into high school athletics and will be entering college next year.

This book was written as *I* prepare to leave Little League— at least as a manager and coach. It is certainly not because I have lost the love of teaching kids how to win and lose and to have fun in their Little League careers; it is simply a recognition that I have had more than my share of satisfac-tion and pleasure over 20 years with three sons in the unique relationship that coaching your child's team provides. But I think it would be selfish of me to continue, at the expense of depriving another parent of that same opportunity.

I am reasonably sure this will be my last book on Little League, because I think I have said it all in two. And whether you read one or both, I hope something will be added to your pleasure and your child's fun in making the most of your respective Little League careers.

1

DRILLS FOR HITTING PRACTICE

Frequently a parent will ask how to help his child become a better ballplayer. I always reply, "Pitch to him so he can get more batting practice." Of all the drills on the basics of playing baseball, the drill that receives the least time *per player* is hitting, and the reason is understandable. If you have only one backstop and field, you can have only one batter hitting at a time, and if you give each player on a 15-player roster 5 minutes of hitting practice, you will consume an hour and 15 minutes of practice time, during which time the other 14 players are idle.

PERSONAL ATTENTION

Compare that to a parent pitching for an hour; the child will get 12 times the amount of practice in hitting that's available in an average team practice. I have a bucket of balls available to lend to a parent willing to devote the extra time. The parent merely pitches them to the child, and then they will take a break as they retrieve the balls and start the sequence over again.

I have seen more dramatic improvement in hitting than in any other practice drill in Little League with father/son hitting practice. Could two kids achieve the same thing, practicing together, or could an older brother do the pitching? Theoretically, yes, but practice requires a certain discipline, particularly when it gets a little boring. Parents and coaches can impose the discipline more effectively than peers can.

Unfortunately some parents come to me after enduring the frustration of watching their child strike out, time after time, when the season may be half over. Consequently, I have a parents' meeting, urging dads especially to attend, before the season begins. That's when I ask for volunteer coaches, umpires, telephone committee members, concession stand workers, and the like. I introduce the parents to each other, since many are strangers to each other, and encourage them to set up car pools to make the transportation part of being a Little League parent a little easier. I also remind them of the objectives of Little League and the potential problems and pressures that can arise from being a poor Little League parent. Above all, I ask for their participation in some way, if not with the team, then at least with their own child in terms of augmenting team practice with home practice.

With respect to hitting in particular, I warn them of the frustration that a rookie player feels—and that they will feel if their child consistently does poorly at the plate. I tell them of the rookies who have gone through *an entire season without hitting the ball once in a game*; not only failing to get a hit, but failing to hit the ball. And I tell them how a few evenings of having someone pitch a bucket of balls might have helped that rookie.

As a coach, you naturally have to recognize situations where it is impossible for the father/son pitching/hitting practice to take place, e.g., a father's work schedule, a father's lack of athletic coordination, or no father at all. I remember how bad I felt, after urging the boys to have their dads attend the next practice when a boy told me tearfully he had no dad. A coach must be aware of those situations, so he can pair off those players with others whose dads may be willing to pitch to two kids; or you as coach may have to serve as a surrogate dad to give those kids some extra practice. In the case of kids who don't live with their fathers, you may have others in the family who would be willing to fill the role: grandfathers, uncles, neighbors—even friends of the family. If you encourage a boy in that situation to "recruit" such a person, you may end up with a "gem." Usually it will be the adult who brings the boy to practice. If you see him or her stay and watch or always come early, it is a sign that he or she may be willing to help.

THE BASICS

Batting drills don't require a ball field. They require only a wall or fence to pitch into, and an area reasonably free of obstructions to hit into. Even in confined areas, a lot of hitting practice can be achieved from the "coach" tossing the ball underhand from the side and the batter hitting it into a fence or wall (see Figure 1-1). Even an uncoordinated parent can master that.

1-1. Hitting Drill: Coach tosses ball in from side, and batter hits it into fence.

Hitting drills, per se, are not enough if they aren't practicing the basics of hitting. In fact, they can be harmful if they allow a boy to repeat bad batting habits. Consequently, it is important that the parents, as well as the coaches, understand the basics of hitting that must be taught and then made mandatory in hitting drills.

Figures 1–2, 1–3, and 1–4 show a total of 31 checkpoints of hitting in the four-stage sequence. That might look intimidating, but everyone must know them, because it may be the failure to execute just one of them that will cause a strikeout instead of a hit. Even a major-league player in a batting slump will have his hitting coach analyze his swing (via sophisticated videotaping in slow motion) and may discover that carelessness in one of the 31 checkpoints is the cause of his hitting problems.

Since I advocate keeping it simple and making it fun, I recommend initially combining the 31 checkpoints into fewer basics for a coach to check. Mike Powers, Little League coach in St. Matthews, Kentucky, breaks the basics of hitting into just three checkpoints:

1. the legs
2. the head
3. the timing

1-2. Ready!
1. Bat is still.
2. Head is still.
3. Chin is on shoulder.
4. Shoulders are level.
5. Arms are parallel to ground.
6. Bat stays away from body.
7. Fingers are loose.
8. Knees are bent slightly.
9. Toes are on parallel line.
10. Front foot pivots toward pitcher.
11. Weight starts to shift to rear foot.
12. Arms move back.

1-3. Aim!
13. Eyes stay on ball.
14. Bat starts forward.
15. Front foot starts stride.
16. Knees turn inward.
17. Head remains still.
18. Wrists bring bat to level swing.

1-4. Fire!
19. Eyes watch ball hit bat.
20. Wrists snap at impact.
21. Weight shifts to front foot.
22. Swing is level.
23. Shoulders are rounded.
24. Hips shift.
25. Rear knee bends.
26. Rear foot pivots.
27. Back toe remains on ground.
28. Wrists roll after contact.
29. Head remains still.
30. Torso turns with bat.
31. Follow-through is smooth.

Basic 1: Checking the Legs

Just as in pitching, where the whole body must be involved, Mike concentrates on the movement of the legs to force the whole body into the act of hitting. During a good swing, the batter steps toward the pitcher with his front foot and pushes with his back foot to start turning his body. As his body turns, he straightens and braces his front leg in order to control his body movement when his arms and hands come into position to hit the ball.

Many Little League batters (and pitchers) use only their upper body—shoulders and arms. Big, strong players get away with it; they hit home runs and strike out batters without learning the best way to hit or pitch.

By using his legs to help him swing, a batter can swing the bat slower for more accuracy, and putting his body's weight into the movement provides more power. The swing should

1-5. The batter is using his legs to get the body to turn forward with a slow, strong motion.

1-6. The "Texas two-step" teaches batter to use legs and body in swing.

be quickly developed to the point that the batter turns his shoulders and hips back and uses his legs to get the body to turn forward with a slow, strong motion (see Figure 1–5). The batter is using the big muscles of the legs, hips, and shoulders to pull his arms and hands into position to hit. This pulling action is more powerful and controlled than the pushing action of using the upper body alone.

To demonstrate the sequence of leg and body movement in a swing, Mike Powers uses a simple drill that a player can practice alone. Mike calls it the Texas two-step, and it is shown in Figure 1–6. The batter locks a bat in his arms behind his back. He then steps forward with his front foot (left foot on a right hander) and rotates the back foot (on the ball of the foot) until the heel is pointing at the backstop (in relationship to home plate). The action with the back foot is like grinding out a cigarette or squashing a bug.

The first part of the drill (stepping toward the pitcher) is fairly natural to a batter, unless he is inclined to be a "parachutist" who bails out for fear the ball will hit him. The second part of the drill (pushing and grinding with the rear foot) is something kids have to be taught and drilled until it becomes just as natural for them. That's where the Texas two-step becomes an effective personal drill, because it is impossible to avoid getting the whole body into the act of swinging when a batter, with a bat locked in his arms behind him, steps forward with the front foot and pushes back and grinds with the back foot. Try it, and you will see what I mean.

How often have you seen a major-league batter raise his hand as he comes to bat (to ask the umpire for time), and "dig a hole" for his back foot. You should remind the kids to look for this routine when they are watching a game on TV. With his strong legs, if a major leaguer didn't do that and attempted to step forward with his front foot and push back with his rear foot, he would end up doing an embarrassed split in full view of the fans. To push off with the rear foot, a batter needs something solid to push against, like the back of the hole he has just dug for his rear foot.

Mike Powers has his boys use the Texas two-step routine both in practice and in games before they come to bat. A couple of times in the on-deck circle will remind a batter to use his legs to get his whole body into the act of hitting.

I mentioned the "parachutist" who wants to bail out of the batter's box to avoid being hit with a pitched ball. Each year, every Little League team will have at least one rookie with the problem. Shame on the coach who doesn't correct it!

If you have a player with this problem, there is no point in trying to teach anything else about batting until you correct the problem. So long as his concentration is on how to avoid being hit, he will not concentrate on anything else. Parents sometimes look shocked when I use my drill to correct this problem with their sons. I lay a bat, parallel to the plate, behind him and warn him that if he tries to bail out and steps on that bat, he may break his leg. If he still bails out by stepping over the bat, I lay down two or three bats, until his

1-7. Bats on ground behind batter teach him or her to stride toward pitcher and not "bail out."

fear of breaking his leg becomes greater than his fear of getting hit with the ball (see Figure 1–7). Then he stands in the box and you can start concentrating on his stepping toward the pitcher with his front foot, while he pushes and grinds with his rear one. I have tackled the bailing out problem with many boys, without one broken leg. The solution will not always be permanent, however. If any player actually gets hit painfully with a pitched ball, watch out for the tendency to bail out the next time he comes to bat.

Basic 2: Head Still, Eyes on the Ball

As a drill to demonstrate this basic, take the position as a batter and have the player you are teaching stand on the pitching mound, facing you. As you go through the motion of swinging at an imaginary ball, ask him to watch your head. Even though your arms, wrists, shoulders, torso, and feet move as you go through the motions of hitting, your head remains still. Only when you have hit the ball does your head turn to the right and focus on first base as you break for that base. (In the process, you are teaching him not to watch the batted ball, which could slow down his dash for first base.)

Then tell him to pretend the emblem on his cap is the ball and to watch your eyes as you again go through the act of hitting. With a player of average size, the emblem on his cap will be in your strike zone and your eyes will be riveted on it as you swing through the imaginary ball. Have the player on the mound take your place at bat, and another player take his place, facing him. By pairing off the kids in this way, after you have shown them the drill, they can take turns in this pretend drill of hitting the ball, while you go up and down the line checking their form. Let them critique each other, too, because in spotting the mistakes a teammate is making, a player will mentally correct that mistake in himself.

Having a batter focus on the emblem of the cap of the "pretend pitcher" will help teach following the ball in from the pitcher, since the emblem is about the size of a baseball.

You can then expand this drill with the use of whiffle balls. Have the pitcher move toward the plate to the point where he can throw a straight ball—one that doesn't drop. Then have the batter concentrate on tracking the ball with his eyes. First he focuses on the cap emblem to get the distance range, then as the pitcher goes into his windup, the batter should focus on the shoulder of the pitcher's pitching arm, since the pitched ball will be released from above that shoulder. As the ball is released, the batter needs to attach his eyes to the ball and track it all the way in. His head remains still; only his eyes move as they follow the ball.

Some major-league hitters, the first time at bat against a

pitcher, will "take" the first pitch, even if it's a strike. It is a tracking exercise for them in concentrating on the pitching motion, the release spot where they pick up the ball, the movement and speed of the ball. They will track the ball right into the catcher's mitt. Their eyes are recording all of this information, so they will be ready for the next pitch. You will hear baseball announcers comment on the "good eyes" of a particular hitter. He seldom strikes out and rarely goes for a bad pitch, because he has mastered the skill of tracking the ball with his eyes.

Another drill to help a batter's tracking ability is to have him stand in the batter's box with a pitcher pitching and a catcher catching. Although he has a bat, and wears a batting helmet, the batter only practices tracking the ball and calls out "ball" or "strike" as the ball approaches the plate. The catcher (or an umpire) can audit his calls, and if the boy is consistently calling them wrong, then he obviously has a problem in tracking the ball accurately.

When a parent is practicing with a child, the parent can go through all of these drills before actually starting to pitch. If, in the tracking drill, the batter calls balls and strikes accurately, he is then ready for some actual hitting practice. It is easy to tell if he is tracking the ball well in a hitting drill, because he will be hitting the "sweet spots," that is, the center of the fat part of the bat will be hitting the center of the ball.

A batter who is not tracking well will be hitting the ball down the handle of the bat, foul-tipping it, missing it, or taking strikes. If this is happening, he needs to go back to the tracking drill, without swinging the bat. Try cutting the toe out of a brightly colored sock, and fitting the open-ended sock on the "hot spot" of the bat. Then the sound will indicate whether the ball is being hit with the fat part of the bat.

Basic 3: Timing

To make the point on the importance of timing, I use the analogy of a pheasant hunter who has to go through the three steps of "ready, aim, fire," but before that last step, must determine in a split second whether the bird he has flushed is a cock or a hen. If a cock (a strike) he fires; if a hen (a ball), he pulls back.

If his tracking is accurate, the batter will know if it's a ball or a strike, but if a strike, how does he know where to meet the ball? The answer is out in front of the plate, and the batter must be made to understand that, since a logical assumption would be to hit the ball over the plate. How often have you called to a batter who took a called strike, "Hey Joe, that ball was *over the plate*"?

I have seen few batters in Little League who swing too early; many, many who swing too late. This, combined with players' assumption that they should hit the ball when it's over the plate, may explain why there are so many strikeouts in Little League.

Timing is a mental factor. Any pheasant hunter can squeeze the trigger of a gun when following a moving bird, but only the hunter who squeezes it at the right moment will have pheasant for dinner. So it is with hitting a baseball. If the batter is going to meet the ball in front of the plate, then he must be able to start his swing soon enough to have it reach its peak of speed and power as the ball arrives in front of the plate. Only practice will condition the perfect timing.

One of the best drills to teach how to hit the ball out front

1-8. Pepper drill teaches batter to hit ball out front.

is "pepper." It is a fun drill that combines quickness of hitting and quickness of fielding (see Figure 1–8). Usually three infielders are spread out in a half circle and pitch the ball (at slow speed), as soon as fielded, back to the hitter. Since the ball is coming slowly, the batter can time his swing to hit the ball on the fat of the bat, out in front. The repetition of this hitting the ball out in front will condition the batter on timing all of his swings to meet the ball at that point.

Mike Powers gives this additional tip on timing: "When the pitcher turns his shoulder, the batter should turn his." The last thing the pitcher does in his windup, before he starts coming toward the plate with the ball, is turn his shoulder toward the plate (left shoulder for a right-handed pitcher). That's the point at which the batter should be turning his shoulder (left shoulder for a right-handed batter) and getting set to come forward with his bat.

THE LEVEL SWING

A tape recorder at a batting drill would probably record the coach's words "level swing" many times. It is obviously what every coach wants batters to do. For a Little Leaguer, however, getting a bat that starts in a semi-vertical position into a level position, parallel to the ground, is more easily said than achieved. When you have told him that the strike zone is from armpits to knees, a vertical distance of several feet, the rookie would be excused if he didn't understand how he could execute a level swing in both the highest and lowest planes of the strike zone. Of course, the answer is that he must adjust his whole body, bending his knees, while keeping his shoulders and elbows level, so his swing will naturally be level.

A drill mentioned before, and shown in Figure 1–1, that will allow a coach (or parent) to audit a child's level swing is the drill where the coach tosses the ball from the side and the batter hits it into a fence. The coach should purposely toss the ball in at different heights within the strike zone to see whether the batter adjusts his body to allow for a level swing. This is also a good drill to practice hitting the ball in front of the plate, since the coach can control his throw to make sure it is in a plane that is in front of the plate.

Coaches will differ in their opinions of position of the feet, elbows, shoulders, and hands of a batter waiting for the pitch, yet they all agree that a swing should be level (parallel to the ground). I recommend the "parallel in–parallel out" approach as the easiest to remember.

The 31 checkpoints noted in Figures 1–2 through 1–4 can be simplified into basics a child can remember. The parallel rules are:

1. *Toes on a line parallel to the plate*—That should mean the batter hits up the middle, which is a good place to hit the ball. Trying to teach a Little Leaguer how to position hits is expecting him to achieve a higher level of baseball prematurely.
2. *Shoulders parallel*—Dipping the shoulders will move the head and make a level swing impossible.
3. *Elbows parallel*—If elbows are level going into the swing, they are more likely to be level coming out of the swing.
4. *Chin parallel to shoulders*—Touching the shoulder with the chin will keep it parallel and prevent the head from moving.
5. *Arms parallel*—Arms should be parallel to the body and away from it before the swing; they should be parallel to the ground as they are extended in a level swing.

That may seem like an oversimplification of the batting swing, but the "parallels rule" is easy to remember—certainly easier than the 31 checkpoints. It is the coach's job to remember the 31 checkpoints, and once the player has mastered the basics of hitting, to start refining the checkpoints in a gradual process of helping him become a better batter. If you teach the average 9- or 10-year-old rookie just to make contact with the ball, you will have done your job as a coach. As he gains in the confidence that he *can* hit the ball, he will be eager to learn the further steps that will make him a good hitter.

CONFIDENCE

The biggest obstacle for a Little League batter to overcome in order to be a good hitter is not learning the mechanics of a good swing, but gaining self-confidence. Many beginning Little Leaguers have an exaggerated fear of the ball and a low estimate of their own ability.

It seems that Little League players gain their confidence all of a sudden. When a player gains confidence, it is like having a new hitter on the team. Almost immediately he begins to hit the ball twice as well as he did before, and he does it without learning anything new about the mechanics of the swing.

The biggest challenge for the Little League manager and coach is to help a young player to gain confidence. In games you need to let him know that you support him and all you expect of him is that he try hard. When he makes a good play or gets a hit, show your appreciation.

In practices you can help the young player to be better able to deal with his fear of the ball, as well as to teach him how not to tense up and be unable to swing at good pitches.

Mike Powers teaches three things to help a batter overcome his exaggerated fear of the ball:

1. Admit that he is afraid of the ball. He is not weak or alone because he is afraid of the ball. Everyone who plays baseball, including the major leaguers, are afraid of being hit by the ball.
2. Learn how to avoid being hit by a pitch. On an inside pitch that could hit the batter, the batter should continue turning his shoulders back until he is facing away from the pitcher, lower his head and fall to the ground. By turning this way he can only get hit in the buttocks or the back of his legs. (The batter should never turn to face the pitcher to avoid being hit.)
3. The most important thing the batter can do to avoid being hit by a pitch is to keep his eyes on the ball by tracking it all the way from release to the bat. The human reflexes are amazing. It is rare for a ballplayer to get hurt when truly concentrating on the ball.

To help the player avoid tensing up and taking good pitches, in addition to dealing with the fear of the ball, I teach the player to begin making slight movements. I begin with the basic idea of getting movement in the batter's box and continue to refine and teach it as he advances.

The basic idea is not to stand rigidly in the batter's box. The batter should make continuous slight movements with each part of his body—shifting his weight slightly from one leg to the other, making short turns with his hips and shoulders, and making short practice swings to keep his arms and hands loose. I begin by suggesting to the batter that he "stay loose" by moving a little while waiting for the pitch.

I also get him to start his swing early in order to be ready to hit when the pitch is a strike. I tell him to turn his shoulders back when the pitcher turns his shoulders back and to step when the pitcher steps. To practice this I start by using a whiffle ball and throw from a short distance, then have him take batting practice from a coach who is pitching easy from a short distance, and gradually move toward having him hit from a player throwing at full speed.

With all batters, I refine these movements into the basic four steps of a good swing:

1. Get loose. While the pitcher is getting ready and starting his windup, the batter should be making slight movements to keep all of his muscles loose and ready to fly into action. He moves his feet "inside his shoes"—he moves slightly back and forth (toward the pitcher) without lifting the balls of his feet, and raises and lowers his heels as he shifts his weight. His hips and shoulders turn back and forth slightly as his weight shifts. He makes short practice swings.
2. See the target. His eyes are preparing to track the ball. He looks at the letter on the pitcher's cap to get the distance, then finds the top of the shoulder on the pitcher's throwing arm and watches for the ball to be released. He locks his eyes on the pitch as soon as it is released.
3. Cock the gun. He has refined what he learned as a

beginner to turn his shoulders back when the pitcher turns his shoulders. Now he can wait until the ball is released before he turns his shoulders back. In order to develop inertia (he will swing the bat like a carpenter drives nails— the swing in one smooth motion back and then through), he moves the bat from his chest to the batter's slot. As he turns his shoulders back, he steps with his front foot. On every pitch, he steps with his front foot, and his hips and shoulders are ready to start turning.

4. Pull the trigger. When he makes the decision to swing, he will maintain good eye contact with the ball and start his swing by grinding his back foot and feeling the pulling action of his body as his hands approach the area in front of the plate where he will make contact. To make contact with the ball, he brings his arms, then hands, and then the bat, through the hitting area. Then, his head stays down as he follows through.

BUNTING DRILLS

The best way to teach a rookie confidence, and help overcome his fear of being hit by a pitched ball, is to teach him how to bunt. In the correct bunting position, with both toes pointing at the pitcher, he has a full view of the ball, and is able to track it best. The bat should make contact with the ball in front of the plate, as explained earlier, and it is much easier to time this when bunting. The ball should hit the fat part of the bat, as explained earlier, and this is also much easier to accomplish in bunting. And, of course, proper timing in contacting the ball with the bat is important, and the reasons for failure to make contact (e.g., swinging too late, taking eyes off the ball) are more obvious in bunting.

Too often when a coach is trying to analyze a hitter's problems in a normal pitching/hitting drill, the action is too fast to pick up the problems. In bunting, this is much easier. The batter whose timing is off in bunting will have a timing problem in hitting; the batter who bails out when bunting will have a serious problem with fear of the ball, and so on.

1-9. Bunting action catches ball hitting fat part of bat in front of plate. Note correct position of hands and feet. (Try not to notice closed eyes.)

On the positive side, the batter who can consistently meet the ball when taught to bunt will gain the confidence that is so important in learning to be a hitter (see Figure 1-9).

A simple drill is with two players facing each other. They stand facing each other about 20 feet apart, one the batter, the other the pitcher. The batter assumes the bunting position: toes in a line pointing toward the pitcher, knees slightly bent, hands up on the bat far enough to control its direction, and upper hand cupped behind the bat.

Have the pitcher start with underhand tosses until the

hitter is bunting the ball back to him consistently. Then have the pitcher throw overhand, but at half speed. When they have mastered the drill, they will be playing a modified form of pepper, and can have fun keeping count of how many times they can keep the ball in play. The boys rotate positions so each has a turn at both positions.

HITTING DRILLS

One of the most effective hitting drills is the two-player drill illustrated in Figure 1–10. It requires only a backstop or a fence to hit against. One player or a coach tosses the ball in from the side, and the batter hits it into the fence. It is better done with two players so the coach can watch and analyze the batter's swing.

Another variation of this drill uses a table. The batter stands on the table facing the backstop, and the "pitcher," lying on the ground, throws the ball up in a vertical plane for the batter to hit. It teaches a batter balance, because if he strides too far or swings off balance, he risks falling off the table. (Naturally, a coach should be standing by to prevent this.)

1-10. Two-player hitting drill. They take turns hitting and tossing balls in from side.

Drill with a Pitching Machine

If your league is fortunate enough to have a pitching machine, by all means use it. However, it does take away one important element in teaching a boy to hit: tracking the ball and perfecting the timing from the pitcher's windup and release.

Our league purchased its first pitching machine toward the end of a season, so it really got its first use during All-Star practice. These boys, the best in the league, were pounding the ball consistently when batting against the machine, but were much less effective when facing a pitcher who pitched no faster than the machine. We reluctantly had to acknowledge that they might have gone to the Little League World Series if they had only had to bat against pitching machines!

The pitching machine has the great advantage of throwing strikes consistently, so a batter can get many more chances to connect with the ball in a given period of time than against a live pitcher. With the machine, you can time the hitting practice sequence and be reasonably sure that every player gets an equal amount of time at bat.

Start the machine at a slow speed with each batter to let him get the feel of hitting, and gradually speed it up to the average speed of pitching in your league (probably never more than 50 m.p.h.). Don't be tempted to set the dials at anything but a fastball, because the speed required to effect a machine-made curve or other trick pitch is greater than Little Leaguers should be facing.

Some coaches recommend the operator of the machine faking a windup for more realism, but it is never the same as facing a pitcher.

Drills with the Batting Tee

Boys like to feel the bat hitting the ball. Nothing improves their batting confidence more. It is the rare rookie who can't connect with a ball that is sitting on top of a batting tee. If he can't, he has serious batting problems that will require some personal coaching.

1-11. One-player hitting drill off tee. Coach Glen Prezocki stresses importance of level swing with lead arm.

When a batter hits the ball off the tee, the coach can check all of the basics: head still, level swing, good stride, and so on. Even bunting form can be checked (see Figure 1-11).

A fun drill, using the batting tee and combining hitting, base running, and fielding, is to have actual intersquad games with the batting tee. The boys will enjoy this kind of practice, because there is lots of action and some competition.

PITCHING/HITTING DRILLS

As the commercial says, "There's nothing like the real thing." A coach can pitch in hitting drills, and the temptation is great, since he will have better control, but it isn't the real thing unless you have a coach who is the same size as a Little Leaguer and pitches at the same speed.

To make it good practice for pitchers as well as hitters, I make the first pitcher warm up well before the session starts, and have a second pitcher warming up to take his place after every five batters (the average number of batters a Little League pitcher faces in an inning).

Many coaches will tell a batter in pitching/hitting drill to bunt three and hit three. But that isn't the real thing. I have them take a turn at bat, with an umpire calling balls and strikes, and either hit the ball, strike out, or walk. To avoid wasting time with horseplay on the bases, the batter goes as far as he can go if he hits the ball, but then comes back to the dugout and gets in line to hit again. The practice will move much faster, and will confine itself to pitching, hitting, and fielding. You can expand it at another time to become a full practice session, involving stealing and base running, but if your objective is to provide the maximum real-thing batting drill, then let the kids just keep coming to the plate and encountering the same situation they will have every time they come to bat in a game. If they get used to the real thing, they will be more relaxed when it happens in a game.

2
DRILLS FOR PITCHING PRACTICE

In team practice, a coach has the same problem in drilling pitchers as hitters: a coach can only work with one player at a time. For that reason I try to find a pitching coach who spends all of his time, *in every practice*, working with the pitchers one at a time. Unless he is willing to be the catcher in these pitching drills, which is a physically demanding assignment, he will have to have some help, either from another parent/coach, or from catching prospects on the team.

Naturally, not every player on your team will be a potential pitcher. Many will want to be who shouldn't, and a few will have no desire. Sometimes a player you initially overlooked will surprise you.

Your best pitcher, if you have a good defensive team, will always be the one who can put his pitches in the strike zone the greatest percentage of the time. He needn't have a blazing fastball, or change-up, or curve—just a ball of any description that finds the strike zone.

Last season, because of rainouts, we were faced with playing the third game in a week back to back to the second game. Since the third game was against the weakest of the three teams, my pitching strategy was to pitch my number 1 pitcher in the first game, number 2 pitcher in the second game, and number 3 pitcher in the third. However I hadn't counted on the second game going into extra innings. With the score tied at the end of six innings, and with my top two pitchers having used up their six innings of eligibility for the week, I was faced with either pitching a rookie in the extra innings and still holding my number 3 pitcher for the next day's game, or using the number 3 pitcher in the second game, realizing that he would then be ineligible to pitch the third game. I have always followed the philosophy of "go for the game you're playing, and don't hold back for tomorrow's game," so we pitched our number 3 pitcher in the extra-inning game and won. Ironically, even though he only had to pitch one inning, he was ineligible to pitch the next day.

Since we played only two scheduled games a week, and a maximum of three in case of a rainout, I had been complacent about grooming only three pitchers. Our 10-team league was well balanced, and all of the games were close, so I did not have the opportunity to give any rookie pitchers a chance to pitch. Now I was faced with having to pitch one (or more) rookies the next day for the first time. I decided on whom to pitch by having a contest among the 4 potential pitchers to see who could pitch the most strikes in 20 tries. The boy I least expected to do well turned out to be the best by far. Because he was big and inclined to be clumsy, and had been inept as a hitter or a fielder, I had essentially written him off as much of a contributor to the team his rookie year.

I wish the story had the happy ending of the rookie pitcher winning the game for us the next day, but we lost. However, we lost on walks, not hits, because nearly every strike the rookie pitcher put over the plate that the other team hit resulted in an out. The fact that he didn't have good enough control in his rookie baptism as a pitcher was more my fault than his; I should have realized his potential earlier and had him practice with my other pitchers. I learned two important lessons from this experience:

1. Train at least four pitchers to be eligible to pitch at any time.
2. Give every boy on the team with the desire to pitch an opportunity to try out as a pitcher.

CHOOSING YOUR PITCHERS

I would recommend the drill we used in the "panic" situation just described to choose your potential pitchers in preseason practice. But don't just use it once; use it on successive days, keeping the cumulative stats of balls and strikes thrown. It will provide the pitchers with competition and incentive to practice on their own, keeping their own ball/strike statistics, until they can consistently throw in the strike zone. It will also sort out for you the boys with a casual interest in pitching from those who are dedicated. The latter, sometimes with the help of an equally dedicated dad or other assistant, will go through his pitching drills every day, and not just during team practice. In my 20 years in Little League, the only pitchers who went on into higher levels of baseball were those with that kind of dedication—usually with someone at home willing to help.

As a boy, I remember reading about the Hall of Fame pitcher Bob Feller, practicing his control on his family's farm. He took an old car tire, hung it from a tree limb in front of the barn and practiced for hours throwing into the strike zone—the center of the tire. To your dedicated pitchers, this might be a good drill at home if they have a tree limb conveniently located. An old tire and a piece of rope could be the makings of another Bob Feller.

Ideally you should have 2 12-year-olds (the maximum you can use in a week, per Little League rules), 2 11-year-olds, and 2 10-year-olds as potential pitchers. Practically speaking, however, you can't give 6 pitchers enough work to sharpen their pitching skills if you only play 2 games each week. So I would recommend concentrating on your 4 best pitchers, so long as only 2 are 12-year-olds.

Like me, you may get into the frustrating situation of

having 3 12-year-old pitchers of nearly equal ability as the season begins. If you also have a good 11-year-old pitcher, it makes the problem even more frustrating, since he will get less pitching time if you elect to alternate your 3 12-year-olds, with one having to skip every third week. My recommendation is to get the kids and their parents together preseason, and explain that the Little League rules prevent your using more than 2 12-year-old pitchers in a week, so you must narrow down the choice to 2 and will do it in the fairest way possible: by comparing their statistics (walks, hits, runs, strikeouts, fielding errors, etc.) in preseason practice games. I would schedule as many preseason practice games as possible and work the 3 12-year-olds until you can reach a decision. The child not selected, and his parents, will understand why and how the decision was made. It will avoid morale-harming dissension on the part of a parent who assumes the child was discriminated against.

One other basic rule in choosing your pitchers: Choose the big kids. Since you won't have the device the major-league teams have to measure the speed of a fastball, you have to assume that the bigger they are, the faster they pitch. You can teach a big pitcher control, but you can't teach a small pitcher speed. This may seem to contradict my earlier statement that the best pitcher is the one who has the best control. I'll still stand by that statement, but if you have to choose between two pitchers with equal control, pick the big one.

PITCHING DRILLS

The drill for choosing pitchers (keeping cumulative totals of strikes and balls thrown in practice) should be continued after your pitchers are chosen, because now you have to rank your chosen pitchers on dependability. Keep daily records to measure their progress. Then start keeping a record of strike position, differentiating between a low strike (belt to knees) and a high strike (belt to armpits).

It is well known that a low pitch is more desirable for these two basic reasons:

1. It is harder to hit.
2. If hit, it will usually result in a ground ball.

There's the old joke about the stranger in New York City who asked someone, "How do you get to Carnegie Hall?" The answer was "Practice, practice, practice!" A coach of mine paraphrased it to "How do you get to be a good ballplayer?" with the same answer.

There is no position in baseball where daily practice is more important in sharpening a ballplayer's skills than the pitching position.

You hear of a pitcher's rhythm, and it is particularly important to a Little League pitcher, awkward about pivoting on a pitcher's rubber, to develop a rhythm that becomes comfortable and automatic. Have you ever seen a bullpen in a major-league park without two pitching rubbers—one for the right-handed relief pitcher and one for the leftie? If just throwing the ball were the only important part of warming up, then the practice rubber would be superfluous. In fact, the whole process of winding up, pivoting the front foot on the rubber, pushing off the rubber, and following through is basic to the pitching rhythm.

Does your Little League ballpark have any practice pitching rubbers? If not, you are not providing your pitchers with one of the necessary tools for pitching drills. If the infield is being used for fielding or batting practice, then your pitchers obviously cannot use the regular pitching rubber for their drills. The four parts of a pitcher's rhythm that must be developed are shown in Figures 2–1 through 2–5.

Mike Powers teaches his pitchers to practice their rhythm even when they are passing the ball to loosen up for practice. He breaks down the four parts of the pitching motion as follows:

1. *Extend and raise the throwing arm.* I have the player catch the ball and turn sideways. Then he puts his throwing hand in the glove and moves his hands toward his chest. As his hands get to his chest, he takes the ball out of the

2-1. Pitcher starts his windup.

2-2. Rubber foot pivots as pitcher finishes windup.

2-3. Whole body is involved as front leg comes up and back bends.

2-4. Front foot strides, rear foot pushes off rubber, back is bent, and ball is thrown from "center field."

2-5. Complete follow-through with rear foot coming forward to assume fielding position.

glove and extends and raises his throwing arm. I tell him to reach for the center-field flag; I describe this as "long arming" (or making the arm "long" before throwing the ball).

2. *Step with the left foot.* I instruct the pitcher to keep his left knee bent and to land on the ball of his foot. I also have him point the toes of his left foot toward the target. After he learns to do this, I draw two interconnecting lines in the dirt. One line is the size of the pitching rubber, and the other is a straight line from the middle of the pitching rubber toward the target. I have the pitcher place his right foot on the right side of the pitching rubber and then land with his left foot on the line that was drawn toward the target.

3. *Push off the rubber.* This movement involves rotating on the ball of the right foot and then pushing the weight forward with the toes. I teach this movement by having the pitcher compare rotating on the ball of the foot to grinding out a cigarette butt on the sidewalk. The pitcher grinds the ball of the foot and then pushes his weight forward with his toes.

4. *Lean forward.* I explain that the pitcher needs to lean forward to throw a low strike. I have him stand sideways to the target, spread his feet and bend his knees, and extend and raise his throwing arm. Then he does only two things to throw: He pushes off the rubber and then leans forward.

After the pitcher learns these basic movements, he can pitch from the mound. He now understands the important movements of the delivery and will be able to appreciate why he needs to make a correct windup. I then teach him the full sequence of the pitch from the stance to the fielding position.

Balance is very important to a pitcher's rhythm. There are three points in the delivery where balancing drills can be helpful:

1. *The flamingo*—This is Mike Powers's term to make the analogy between standing on the pivot leg with the other

2-6. Holding pitcher's rear foot in practice drill forces use of whole body in pitching.

knee raised waist high in the position of the flamingo, standing perfectly balanced on one leg. Having your pitchers practice being flamingos will help them with this important balance phase of pitching.

2. *The sitting position*—This is when the left knee (on a right-handed pitcher) is raised and his arm is going back toward center field. At this point he should bend his right knee to get his body in a lowered position—like he is sitting down.

3. *Using the back*—You will hear coaches admonishing their pitchers to "use your back," or "use your body"—as opposed to just pitching with the arm. If I see this weakness in a pitcher, I have another player hold his pivot foot as he comes around. There is no way, with this restriction, that he can pitch the ball without bending his back and following through. Figure 2–6 shows this drill being used on a left-handed pitcher.

CHART 1. PITCHER COVERING FIRST BASE DRILL

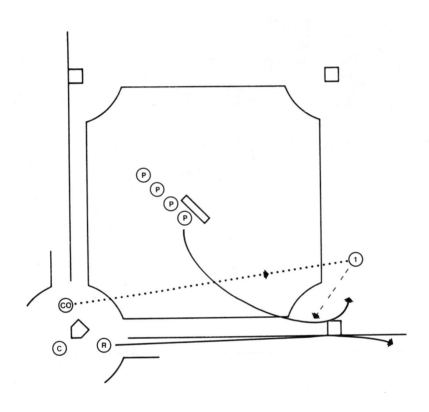

Key:

(P) Pitcher

(C) Catcher

(1) 1st Baseman

(R) Runner

(CO) Coach

•••••••••••••▶ Batted Ball

– – – – – –▶ Underhand Toss

——————▶ Player Running

PITCHER AS FIELDER

You have little to fear as long as your pitcher is pitching consistently in the strike zone, and you have a good infield.

You often hear the phrase "a good infield backing up the pitcher," but in fact *the pitcher is part of the infield.* So if your pitcher is not a good fielder, you do not have a good infield. A savvy coach of an opposing team will notice a pitcher who is off balance when he finishes his pitch, and will have his team bunt. Nothing will unnerve a team (or a coach) more than to have the batter hit an easy bounce back to the pitcher and then have the pitcher throw the ball three feet over the first baseman's head.

Chart 1 shows a drill for pitchers learning how to cover first base on a grounder to the first baseman. In the drill, you line up your pitchers on the mound and let them take turns circling to the inside of the base and taking the underhand throw from the first baseman. If you have more than one first baseman, you can rotate at that position, too, as the coach hits grounders to the first base position.

A good fielding drill for a pitcher—involving pitcher, catcher, and first baseman—is this: Have the pitcher pitch (as he normally would), and have the catcher throw grounders to the left of the mound, or to the right, or directly back (but in no sequence, so the pitcher will not know where the ball is coming). Have the pitcher field the ball and throw to first.

Another fielding drill, involving the same three players, is to have the catcher throw a ball to the right side, out of reach of the pitcher, which the first baseman must field, and have the pitcher cover first. It is important to teach the pitcher to circle back into the infield when he touches first, in order to avoid a collision with the base runner, who is running up the line on the foul side of the first base line (see Figure 2–7).

For variation and to add some reality to the play, add a runner to these drills.

When teaching the "hot-box" drill outlined in Chapter 4, note that *the pitcher is involved as a fielder in every hot-box situation.* He backs up the first baseman in a rundown between first and second; he backs up the third baseman in a

2-7. First baseman at left has tossed ball underhand to pitcher (center) who touched base and is circling back to infield to avoid collision with runner (right).

rundown between second and third; and he backs up the catcher in a rundown between third and home.

A pitcher who does not cover home on a wild pitch or passed ball will make stealing home easy for the opposition. A savvy coach will notice that the pitcher is not covering and tell his base runners to take advantage of the situation. If I see a new opposing pitcher enter the game when I have a runner on third, I will signal that runner to go far off base on every pitch because a new pitcher is likely to be wild and to be too nervous to remember to cover home on a wild pitch or passed ball.

To add another dimension to your pitcher's fielding ability, you can add a runner on third to either of the two drills. Either the pitcher will naturally throw some wild pitches, or the catcher will deliberately let some balls pass to drill the pitcher's ability to do three difficult fielding maneuvers:

1. Cover home plate.
2. Take the throw from the catcher.
3. Tag the runner without dropping the ball.

It is frustrating to see steps 1 and 2 executed, only to have the pitcher fail at step 3. It obviously merits some drilling. How often have you seen a batter walk, steal second, go to third on a wild pitch, and steal home on a passed ball? It happens so often in our league that I figure that two out of three walks are automatic runs. Now do you understand why control is so important in pitchers?

HOW MANY PITCHES?

So far, the only pitch discussed has been the fastball—no curves, change-ups, two-fingered fork balls, or knuckle balls. The omission is deliberate.

Last season I noticed my catcher was having a lot of conferences on the mound, and my pitcher was giving up a lot of walks. Finally I went out and asked them what was happening. The catcher said the pitcher wasn't following his signals. "What signals?" I asked, and he replied, "One finger for a fast ball, two for a curve ball, and three for a change-up." I made these pointed observations to my battery:

- I hadn't taught them to use any signals.
- The pitcher didn't know how to throw a curve ball or change-up!

Seems they had watched a major league game on TV, for which Joe Garagiola was the commentator. Joe, being a former catcher, made quite a story about the importance of signals between catcher and pitcher. So they thought they would give it a try!

If all of the time spent by Little League coaches trying to teach their pitchers how to throw curve balls and other "major-league" pitches was spent on practicing control of the fast pitch, the coaches would win more games. Until a pitcher has mastered rhythm and control, you shouldn't even think about teaching him anything else.

Assuming your pitcher has good control, then teach him a change-up. It is the easiest auxiliary pitch to teach. It should be thrown only when the pitcher is ahead of the batter, that

2-8. Two grips of fastball will cause delivery to differ.

is, on an 0-and-2 or 1-and-2 count. The change-up should only be thrown to good hitters. I have seen too many cases of a weak hitter swinging late on two fastballs, only to have the pitcher throw him a change-up that was exactly the speed that let him meet the ball. Throw a change-up to a good batter, who has to adjust his timing to be able to hit it.

The change-up is thrown just like the fastball, except that the ball is "palmed," whereas the fastball is held on the tips of the fingers. Since the pitching motion is the same, the good hitter has every reason to believe a fastball is coming, and is frustrated to see it "float" in and completely destroy his timing. Getting the float on a change-up is something that only hours of practice will develop. Make sure those hours are not at the sacrifice of the pitcher's control.

Variations of the fastball can be achieved by the pitcher's grip: He can either cross the stitches with his fingers or let them run parallel to the stitches (see Figure 2–8). Have your pitchers practice both ways, and observe the difference in delivery, if any. Sometimes the cross-stitch grip, coupled with a wrist snap at the release, will cause the ball to tail off like a curve ball.

Only when your pitcher has mastered excellent control, a change-up, and grip variations of the fastball, would I consider teaching him how to throw a curve ball. And in no case would I teach him anything but a slow curve, since any other type of pitch used in higher levels of baseball can jeopardize the health of a young arm.

Chances are you won't have to teach a good pitcher how to throw a curve. He will be curious enough to have an older boy show him how, and then will come to you to show off his new-found skill.

The grip for a curve ball is fingers across the seam and the thumb bent underneath. The hand curves "inside out" on the release, with the thumb pushing the ball to give it rotation, and the wrist snapping to give it trajectory. If this sounds complicated, forget it, since the Little League pitcher who can effectively throw a curve ball is rare, and the time spent teaching a pitcher who is not that talented would be better spent on his control.

3

DRILLS FOR DEFENSIVE PRACTICE

In the preceding chapter, I mention the danger of not giving all players a chance to show you what they have, and therefore overlooking a good prospect. This is true not just of the new rookies, but of the returning boys as well. If you predetermine a child's capabilities based on what he did last year, you aren't allowing for the tremendous changes that can occur in a year in size, speed, strength, and coordination. Giving everyone a chance to play every position is important in your early season practices.

TRYOUT DRILL

Give all the players at least one opportunity to try out as a:

- pitcher
- catcher
- first baseman (record the distance he can stretch from his glove to the bag)
- infielder
- outfielder

BASE-RUNNING DRILL

You want to know how fast each player is so that you will know how to coach him as a base runner. Using a stop watch, record his speed from home to first, his speed in stealing second, and his speed in circling the bases. Rather than racing the players against each other, which embarrasses the slower ones, keep an individual record on each player and encourage him to beat his best time in subsequent time trials.

AIM FOR "STRONG UP THE MIDDLE"

The backbone of your defense has to be the up-the-middle positions: catcher, pitcher, second baseman, shortstop, and centerfielder. They should be your strongest, fastest, best-coordinated kids. And they should be the positions where you substitute the least, in order to maintain a strong up-the-middle defense.

Frequently your best pitchers will also be your best short-stops, so if you alternate at that position, it will mean the least disruption of your up-the-middle defense. Your best pitchers may also be good catchers, but since the position of catcher is most prone to injury and is physically demanding, it is better to avoid using pitchers in the catching position. I have seen a boy catch for three innings on a hot day and then be asked to pitch. He obviously will not be at his peak strength after three perspiring innings behind the plate.

AROUND-THE-HORN DRILL

Around the horn is my favorite drill for giving all players a chance to practice at every position. Ideally you should have three coaches, plus yourself, conducting the drill, because it allows everyone to practice at the same time and prevents boredom on the part of watchers. Chart 2 shows how your coaches would line up: one between home and third, hitting grounders to the first and second basemen and fly balls to the rightfielder and right-center fielder; another coach between home and first base, hitting grounders to the third baseman

CHART 2. "AROUND THE HORN" PRACTICE ROUTINE
(using as many as 2 coaches and 15 players)

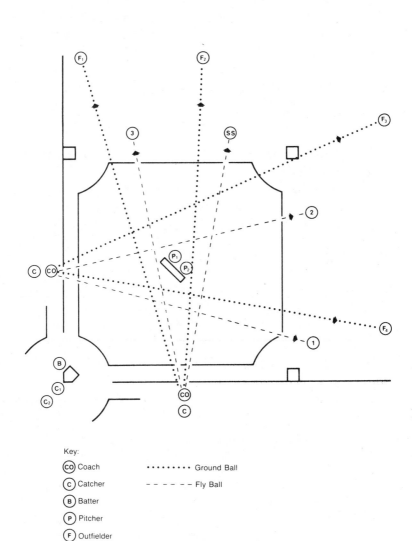

Key:
- (CO) Coach
- (C) Catcher
- (B) Batter
- (P) Pitcher
- (F) Outfielder

· · · · · · · · Ground Ball
– – – – – – Fly Ball

and shortstop and fly balls to the leftfielder and left-center fielder; and a third coach behind home plate, working with the pitchers and catchers. If you are free of any coaching responsibility in this drill, you will have the opportunity to take notes on the performance of each player at each position.

To enable everyone to play every position, rotate the players periodically in the course of the drill. Note that there are 15 positions to hold (including the "pretend batter" working with the pitchers and catchers).

The normal shift in rotating the players is from left to right. To shift from outfield to infield, the sequence is rightfielder to catcher (for coach between home and first) to third base. To shift from infield to outfield, the sequence is from first baseman to catcher (for coach between home and third) to left field.

When evaluating an infielder, check:

- reaction time in moving to the position of the grounder
- ability to field the ball
- speed in getting rid of the ball
- ability to catch the relay from an outfielder
- speed and accuracy in throwing to the catcher

Recognizing that this is an early practice drill, you don't expect perfection, but you look for the raw talent that is coachable and the basic weaknesses that may not be easily coachable, such as fear of the batted ball.

In evaluating an outfielder, check:

- reaction time in going to the position of the fly ball
- ability to position himself accurately
- ability to catch the ball
- speed in getting rid of the ball
- speed and accuracy in throwing to the relay

You can either practice the pitchers and catchers as an independent unit or work them into the infield/outfield sequence. Naturally you will want to work the "pretend batter" into either the pitcher/catcher drill or the infield/outfield drill.

Boredom of players in practice is a serious problem for coaches. Young players will quit your team if they are bored and have something more interesting to do. Invariably the reaction of another coach to watching our round-the-horn drill is to recognize it as a way to prevent boredom, since all players are active and there is variety in what they are practicing.

It should be noted that in preventing boredom by having different things going on to involve all of your players at the same time, there is an obvious risk of injury if the various drills are not well organized and kept as far apart as possible. The "Round the Horn Drill" requires the services of three adult coaches at the same time, and as a safety consideration should not be conducted with any fewer. The same precautions should be exercised in any drills where more than one ball and bat are used at the same time.

AVOID STEREOTYPES

The stereotypes of the big catcher, or the big, left-handed, clumsy first baseman are unfortunate. Since the catcher is one of the key players in the up-the-middle defense, I don't want a big, clumsy boy in that position. Some of my best catchers have been small, quick, "good head" players. Many major-league teams will relegate good hit–poor field players to the first-base position, because plays at first base are so routine. Nothing is routine in Little League, however, and since a much bigger percentage of balls are hit to the right side of the diamond, your first baseman needs to be a good fielder.

Why are many balls hit to the right side of the infield? Because you have inexperienced batters swinging late on fastballs. The advantage of being left-handed is not as great in Little League as in higher levels of baseball, so don't put a boy at first base just because he is left-handed. On the other hand, if he is a good infielder, first base is his best position, since the other infield positions favor right-handed throwers.

The tendency of coaches in early season is to go immediately to the traditional infield drills of hitting to the infielder, who throws to first; hitting to the infielder, who throws to the catcher; double play; and the like. There will be plenty of time for that later. Initially, however, you should spend a lot of time on the round-the-horn drill to evaluate your talent. Rotate the boys frequently, since a lot of throwing is involved and you will get sore-arm complaints if you let the drill continue too long.

When you have established which kids will play infield and which outfield, you can then break your defensive practices into three groups: infielders, outfielders, and pitchers/catchers, preferably with a coach for each group, so that you can roam among all three.

FIELDING TECHNIQUE

It is important initially to establish the correct "set" position for an infielder as the pitcher delivers:

1. Feet spread wider than shoulder width.
2. Balanced on balls of the feet and able to shift weight from side to side.
3. Legs bent and butt low.
4. Hands on knees until pitcher winds up; then hands out, knee-high.
5. Eyes on the strike zone as pitcher releases the ball.

When the ball is hit in his fielding area the infielder must:

1. Move to the ball, charging it if it is a slow roller, or moving to the spot of intercept (see Figure 3–1).
2. Keep body low in order to keep glove low, since the most common infielding error is letting the ball go under the glove.
3. Keep eyes on the ball and "look it into the glove" (see Figure 3–2).
4. Pick the ball out of the glove and sight on the target (see Figure 3–3).
5. Step toward the target while throwing (see Figure 3–4).

3-1. Shortstop moves to the ball.

3-2. Looks the ball into his glove.

3-3. Picks ball out of glove and sights on target.

3-4. Steps toward target as he throws to first.

An infielder's biggest fear is getting hit in the face with a "bad hop." To help overcome this fear and protect against the bad hop, Mike Powers recommends the infielder hold his bare hand above the glove, palm down, so he can stop the bad bounce with his bare hand. It's an excellent tip, because once an infielder is hit in the face with a ground ball, you can count on his being "gun shy" on hard-hit grounders until he forgets the hurt.

A good infielder will show aggressiveness in fielding the ball; he will go after it instead of waiting for it to come to him. It is what coaches call playing the ball and not letting the ball play you. It is part instinct, part training. Players who are aggressive in other ways are also aggressive infielders, and the reverse is also true. The boy who demonstrates a fear of being hit at bat and is always bailing out will normally carry that fear onto the field and will be difficult to coach into becoming a good infielder.

A symptom of fear of getting hit is "side-saddling" the ball—trying to field the grounder by reaching to the side, instead of in front of the body. It is safe, from an injury standpoint, since if the ball takes a bad hop, it will bounce over the glove into the outfield. But it's bad fielding technique, because a bad hop that the body blocks can still be an out or save a run, but a bad bounce over the glove is a hit and possibly an RBI.

INFIELD DRILLS

To teach the basics of the technique of fielding an infield ball, I advocate two-, three-, or four-player drills before going to the standard drill of the coach hitting grounders and the infielder throwing to first. That drill is important, but should be preceded in the early practices of the season with more basic, individualized instruction with drills such as the ones that follow.

The "Alligator"

Mike Powers's invention to teach the boys to keep their

3-5. Right hand above glove, palm down like an alligator.

bare hand above the glove with palm down is called the "alligator." It helps in three ways:

1. It protects against the bad hop.
2. It secures the catch by clamping the bare hand on the ball in the glove.
3. It helps a quick release as the fielder digs the ball out of the glove for the throw.

The reason Mike calls it the alligator is that it is like the jaws of an alligator clamping down on the ball. The analogy helps kids remember the proper technique (see Figure 3–5).

It is a two-player drill, with one player being the infielder, the other the first baseman. The batter rolls the ball to the infielder, he fields it and makes the throw to the first baseman. At first he throws slow rollers directly to the infielder, then increases speed and varies location.

You can have as many boys active in this drill as you have infield ground to use.

The Bouncing Ball

You hear baseball announcers talk about an infielder fielding the ball on the "high hop" or on the "short hop." They are the two ideal points at which to field a bouncing ball—when it is at its highest point or just as it starts to rise. Which way to play the ball is a split-second decision an infielder has to make as he sees the ball coming toward him "on the hop." Only practice will develop both the skill and the judgment necessary to make the play consistently.

In this two-player drill, one player is the infielder, the other the first baseman. The first baseman bounces the ball to the infielder, who fields it and throws to first. Mike Powers suggests starting with rubber balls, which will more closely approximate the kind of bounce a hard-hit baseball would take.

The Dive

Have you ever seen Ozzie Smith, the Wizard of Oz, make one of his dive catches, body parallel to the ground, come down gracefully on both feet, and throw out the runner at first by 10 feet? An infielder needs to be taught to make two kinds of dive catches: the line-drive catch, and the bouncing ball catch.

The dive drill is either a two-player or three-player drill. In a three-player drill, the two infielders can be playing the shortstop and second base positions, and the third player or coach stands between the pitcher's rubber and second base. The third player alternates line-drive throws or bouncing balls to either side of the two infielders, enough out of their reach that they have to dive for them (see Figure 3-6). This is a catching version of the "pepper drill," which is described next, in that part of the drill involves the infielder releasing the ball as quickly as he can back to the thrower. It is a fast-paced drill, guaranteed to tire your participants quickly.

If your infield is very hard, it is better to have the infielders playing back at the edge of the outfield grass, so their dives are cushioned by the grass. This, like a sliding drill, is better

3-6. Coach throws ball out of reach of infielders, who must dive for it.

done after some rain when the infield is soft. However, to prepare for all conditions of infield, all infield drills should be done on varying surfaces to demonstrate the different ways a ball bounces, depending on soft or hard infields. Even major-league controversies have occurred where one team has accused another of having either too hard or too soft a surface. Our All-Star team has played on fields where the infield grass was so high and the infield surface was so soft that it was impossible for a ground ball to get through. The home team was used to playing under those conditions, and had an advantage.

On one field, when we took our All-Star team to practice a day before the game, there appeared to be no pitcher's mound. There was a rubber, but it seemed to be level with home plate. I asked the home-field manager when they were going to construct the mound, and he told me, rather indignantly, that their pitcher's rubber was the Little League prescribed height above home plate and he had the surveyor's certification to prove it. Be that as it may, the fact remained that it had a different look and feel, which the home-team pitchers were used to but the visiting pitchers had difficulty adjusting to.

3-7. Pepper drill: Batter and three infielders try to keep ball in play.

Pepper Drill

The pepper drill is a fun drill that your kids will enjoy. Usually it involves a batter and three infielders (see Figure 3-7), although it can be done with as few as a batter and one infielder. The number of simultaneous drilling groups is limited only by the infield you have available. Even with only one infield, you could have as many as four drills going on simultaneously, as Chart 3 demonstrates. To avoid balls going through the batter and interfering with another group drilling, it is wise to have a catcher backing up each hitter. If you use all the players, you can have as many as 15 practicing at the same time. If you have fewer players, then have fewer infielders per group, which will give each player more balls to field. Naturally you rotate your team members within each group so that all have a chance to field and hit.

The fielders throw the ball back to the batter overhand, but at half speed, and he hits the ball at half strength. The fun of the drill is in keeping the ball in play. To add some competition to the drill, challenge them to see which group can keep the ball in play the longest time. Have them count the number of hit balls before the sequence is broken.

This drill will give not only practice in quick-response fielding, but good eye-hand coordination practice in batting as well.

CHART 3. PEPPER DRILL WITH FOUR GROUPS ON ONE INFIELD

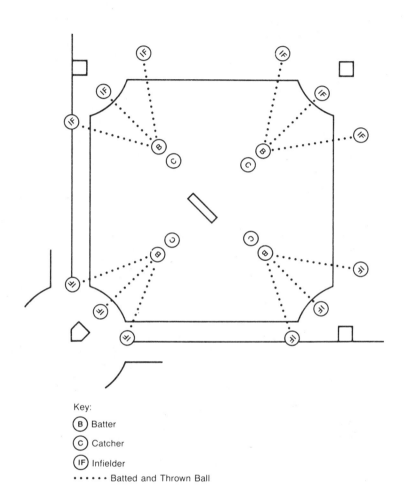

Key:

(B) Batter

(C) Catcher

(IF) Infielder

•••••• Batted and Thrown Ball

CHART 4. POP FLIES TO THE INFIELD

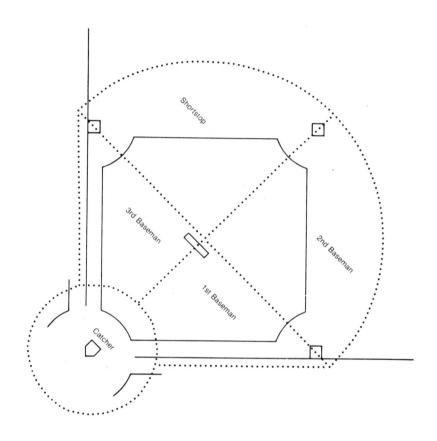

Rules On Borderline Catches

1. Fielder moving backwards gives way to Fielder coming in.
2. Fielder crossing arm in front of body gives way to fielder with arm closer to ball.
3. Always call for ball if it is your catch.

STANDARD INFIELD DRILL

The standard infield drill of a coach hitting in sequence to his infielders is:

1. Throw back to catcher.
2. Throw to first and back to catcher.
3. "One and cover": throw to first, back to catcher, catcher back to infielder covering his base.
4. "Around the horn": throw to first, who throws to second, to short, to third, to home.
5. "Force at second": throw to second baseman or shortstop covering second.
6. "Force at third": throw to third baseman.
7. "Force at home": throw to catcher.

A lot of coaches include a double-play drill, but how many double plays did you see in your league last year? And how many errors on an attempted double play? I would rather concentrate on the force-play drill and not complicate it with the pivot and throw to first to attempt the double play. Remember that the base lines in Little League are only 60 feet, versus 90 feet in higher levels of play, so it is an exceptionally slow runner who cannot beat out a double play.

CATCHING POP-UPS

Chart 4 shows the areas in which various infielders should catch pop-ups. You will note that the pitcher is excluded, and for good reason. He has the two problems of coming off the mound and being off balance to catch a pop-up, which just make the assignment more difficult. It is better to leave him out of it, since the smaller infield in Little League should allow the other five infielders to cover the designated areas easily.

I recommend that you lay down lines, as Chart 4 shows, so your infielders get used to understanding their designated areas for catching pop-ups. Nevertheless, there will be bor-

3-8. Centerfielder, coming in, makes catch rather than short-stop, moving back.

derline cases where these rules should be applied:

1. The fielder coming in should take it, rather than the fielder backing out (see Figure 3-8).
2. The fielder who doesn't have to reach across his body should take it, rather than the fielder who does have to reach across his body. Thus, with all right-handed in-fielders, a borderline pop-up between first baseman and second baseman should be taken by the second baseman; between second baseman and shortstop should be taken by the shortstop; between shortstop and third baseman should be taken by the third baseman (see Figures 3-9 and 3-10).

Naturally, the surest way to avoid collision is for the player who should catch the ball to call out "I've got it," or "Mine," and wave his arms to emphasize with movement (in case his voice cannot be heard). The catcher, who is in a good position to see the play, can help when he sees a potential collision, by

3-9. On borderline catches between first and second basemen, second baseman makes the catch.

3-10. On borderline catches between second baseman and shortstop, shortstop makes the catch.

3-11. Catcher gets rid of mask to determine who should catch pop-up.

calling the name of the boy who should catch the ball, for example, "Joe's catch!" (see Figure 3-11).

The proper catch is with both hands above the face, with the bare hand ready to clamp over the ball as soon as it hits the glove.

A "fungo bat" is good for a coach to use in hitting pop-ups. If he has trouble hitting pop-ups consistently, he can just throw the ball up. Figure 3-12 shows Glenn Prezocki, one of Mike Powers's coaches, using a tennis racket and ball with rookies, who may be gun-shy of catching a hard ball in the beginning practices. I have seen enough rookies get hit on the head with a baseball, because they misjudged it, that Mike's technique with the tennis racket makes sense. Once they have mastered the technique of going to the ball, getting under it, and catching it directly overhead, they can be weaned from the tennis ball to the baseball.

3-12. Coach Glenn Prezocki uses tennis racket and balls to teach rookies to catch fly balls.

FLY-BALL DRILLS

Coaches who just hit fly balls to a disorganized group of boys in the outfield are giving practice only to the more aggressive boys, while risking injury at the same time. Not only can a player be hit in the scramble to catch the fly ball, but if he has to throw the ball many times from the outfield back to the hitter, he is putting a strain on his throwing arm.

That kind of drill also fails to take advantage of the opportunity to coach an outfielder in another important job: making an accurate throw to the relay player.

I recommend an outfield drill involving three to five players and a coach. In a three-player drill, one is the outfielder, one is the relay, and one is the catcher. You can expand it to four or five players by adding one or two outfielders. Figure 3–13 shows the drill with three players and a coach. The coach hits fly balls to the outfielder, varying position and distance. The outfielder throws the ball to the relay, and the relay pivots and throws to the catcher. To add

3-13. Outfielder drill: Coach uses three players in drill to teach catching fly balls, throwing to relay, who throws to catcher. Players rotate positions.

some competition and fun to the drill, I tell the kids to score two points for a catch, one point for a good throw to the relay, and one point for a good throw from the relay to the catcher. Each team of three keeps their point total and compares it with other teams of three.

When you expand the drill to include three outfielders, it is important to coach the importance of backing up each other, so that a ball that gets through one can be quickly retrieved by his back-up outfielder.

Ground balls should also be hit to outfielders, and they should be taught how to block the ball by dropping to one knee and keeping the body in front of the ball. How many times have you seen a routine single turn into a triple or inside-the-park home run because the outfielder let the ball get through and roll to the fence?

SITUATION DRILLS

After the basics have been taught, and your kids have been pegged for certain positions, you should go through team situation drills, such as one out, runner on third, fly to left field. We conduct them using runners to add realism to the drill. In the preceding example, we would have a runner on third base tag up after the catch and break for home. It would test the leftfielder's throwing ability and accuracy, the catcher's catching and tagging ability, and the runner's speed and sliding ability.

The kids enjoy this kind of situation drill using runners, because it is close to real game situations.

Make out a list of all of the various situations and use it in the drill. If you are rained out of a practice, then have a "skull session," using the same list and asking the specific players involved in a particular situation to tell you what they would do.

One of the most popular situation drills that your kids will enjoy practicing is the "hot-box" drill. Since it is a running as well as a fielding drill, we will cover it in the next chapter with the drills for running the bases.

4
DRILLS FOR BASE-RUNNING PRACTICE

Is running so basic that you don't have to teach it? You would think so until you meet your first rookie who runs on his heels or flails his arms as he runs. The basic running form is to lean forward, head down, run on toes, pump arms, eyes straight ahead.

The preceding chapter mentions that I have periodic foot races among the players in early practice, usually by age level, but ultimately to find out who is the fastest team member.

Make the race course 60 feet, tell them it is the distance between home and first, and emphasize that it is like a track meet, with the finish line being first base. Then ask them if they have ever seen a track meet where the runners slowed up as they reached the finish line. Get them to picture in their minds the track star breaking the finish line at full speed, and tell them that's the way you want them to cross first base. Also ask them if they have ever seen a track star, while running, look at anything but the finish line tape. Does he look up in the stands to see if his girlfriend is watching?

I emphasize these two things:

4-1. Base runner has run through first base at full speed.

1. Hit the finish line (first base) at full speed.
2. Never take eyes off first base.

The reason for this emphasis is that the two major problems you will have in teaching kids how to run *through*—not *to*—first base are slowing up as they near first base and looking at the ball as they run up the line.

There is something in the mind of your average rookie that makes him instinctively slow up as he approaches first base, whereas he should run through it on the foul line side at full speed (see Figure 4-1). What makes him slow down may be the mistaken fear that he can be tagged out if he goes too far beyond first base. In any event, it is a common problem with Little Leaguers that I have coached, and it needs to be dealt with early. If, after we have established the principle of running through first base, they slow up in practice sessions, I make them run laps as punishment.

The other natural tendency is to look at the ball instead of first base as they are running up the line. This has a tendency

4-2. First baseman is crowding base, but base runner hits foul line side of first base without breaking stride.

to slow the runner. I kid them about looking at their girlfriends. If they are looking at anyone, it should be the base coach, who will be giving them the windmill sign to keep going if the ball has gone through the outfielder or has been thrown wild to first. Another reason for urging a boy to look only at the base is to avoid injury. Often a first baseman will be forced to crowd the base to take a bad throw (see Figure 4–2), and the baserunner needs to touch the foul line side of the bag to avoid a collision.

The fear of getting caught off base is so great in the minds of many rookies that it inhibits their ability to run the bases. They instinctively stop and hold when they reach a base. We emphasize just the opposite—that a base is something you should leave as soon after you touch it as possible. When you are on base, you leave it on every pitch (as it reaches the plate), and you return to it only if you have to.

RUN-WHEN-YOU-WALK DRILL

We teach the Pete Rose way of getting a walk. He runs to first and takes a turn. In Little League it can mean an extra base if the other team is sleeping. If the catcher or pitcher is not watching the runner, or if the second baseman and shortstop are not covering second base, a savvy runner can run to first, make a turn, and keep on running to second. We have done it many times, and it is worth drilling both as a practice drill and in situation play drills.

SLIDING DRILL

To avoid painful "brush burns" on players' thighs, the sliding drill should be done in a sliding pit (with sawdust) if you have one, or on soft dirt (hose it down well and then loosen it with a rake), or on grass that has been hosed.

These are the sliding pointers that should be stressed:

1. Run close to the ground and slide without breaking stride.
2. Slide feet first with the feet raised off the ground. (The head first slide is not for Little League.) Since metal spikes are not allowed, the raised foot will not hurt the baseman, but may knock the ball out of his glove.
3. Slide on the right hip (body turned away from the throw), hands outstretched for balance.
4. Aim for the center of the base.
5. Relax your legs.
6. Keep hands off the ground.
7. Be ready to scramble to your feet and keep going if the ball went through.
8. If you are safe and the baseman has the ball, call "time" immediately.
9. Don't assume you are out if you heard a call or saw an out sign from the umpire. Infielders have been known to make the call, and umpires have been known to change their call if they saw the tag out and then saw the infielder drop the ball.

STEALING-SECOND DRILL

Most stealing in Little League is on a passed ball or wild pitch. And with some teams, that is the only stealing that is done.

We coach the runner on first to go off two steps on every pitch (as it crosses the plate) and to go off as if he will keep going. If he does that, then he can keep going at full speed if the ball is hit, is pitched wild, or is passed by the catcher (see Figure 4–3).

I will also attempt a steal early in the game to test the catcher. I won't do it with every player, only with the fast ones. That's one of the reasons for drilling with foot races to determine which players are your fastest.

4-3. Runner on first is ready to push off as soon as the pitch crosses the plate.

4-4. Second baseman has position but doesn't have the ball on a steal.

The base-stealing drill is best done when the ground is soft, because the base runners are naturally expected to slide. It should involve pitcher, catcher, pretend batter, runner, second baseman, and shortstop. The pitch is made, the catcher throws (with mask on), the runner breaks and slides, and the shortstop or second baseman makes the tag, with the other backing him (see Figure 4-4). In higher levels of baseball, the second baseman takes the throw with a right-handed batter up, and the shortstop with a left-handed batter. In Little League, I recommend that the manager designate who should take the throw and have him take it in every situation.

STEALING-THIRD DRILL

I don't recommend having a runner steal third, unless on a wild pitch or passed ball, and only then when the ball is well out of reach of the catcher. The distance of 60 feet is just too short a throw from catcher to third baseman for the base runner to be able to beat. I might risk it if I see that a rookie third baseman or catcher has been inserted in the lineup; but it's too rare a play to merit drilling.

STEALING-HOME DRILL

Stealing home is an important play to drill, both offensively and defensively. Offensively, the base runner should be coached to go off the base as soon as the pitch reaches the plate, and keep on going on a wild pitch or passed ball. It is important that he (and the coach) observe:

- the position of the third baseman
- the action of the catcher in returning the pitch to the pitcher
- whether the pitcher covers home on a wild pitch or a passed ball

If the third baseman plays well off the base, with a runner on third, the runner can go down the line on every pitch as far as the third baseman is playing off the base. If the third baseman is well off the base and the catcher makes no attempt to force the runner back to third, the runner can break for home from his position down the line, as soon as the catcher releases the ball back to the pitcher. While the runner is running and sliding into home, the pitcher has to catch the ball and throw it back to the catcher, and the catcher has to make the tag. In most cases, it is no contest, with the runner scoring.

In a game last season, we had the winning run on third base, bottom of the sixth with two outs and a weak hitter at bat. I signaled to the base runner on third to take a chance. He started down the line on the next pitch, and the catcher started up the line to meet him. When the catcher forced our runner back to third, he was two-thirds of the way up the line to third base, and no one was covering home. As soon as he released the ball to the pitcher who was on the pitcher's mound, our runner broke for home, scored standing up, and the ball game was won!

We have a drill we call "zebra," for lack of a better name. It is for a situation with a runner on third, two out, and a weak hitter at bat. The base runner deliberately breaks for home on the next pitch, forcing a run down. We gamble on his scoring by outwitting the catcher and third baseman in the rundown, since the chances are the weak hitter would not have scored him anyway. Our record on scoring in the zebra situation was two out of three times, which made it worth the gamble.

Another situation that should be coached is watching what the catcher does when he has to go back to the screen to retrieve a passed ball or wild pitch. He may recover it too soon, and the pitcher cover home too quickly, to risk a steal. However, when the catcher sees that the runner on third is not breaking for home but holds on to the ball at the screen until the pitcher retreats to the mound and then releases it, the base runner can steal at the moment of release, because the catcher, with all of his equipment on, has to run back to the plate, catch the ball, and make the tag.

"HOT-BOX" DRILL

The hot-box drill is probably the most popular; the kids even like to practice it on their own. I can remember visiting my son at the Little League Baseball Camp at Williamsport and noticing a hot-box game going on outside nearly every cabin during their free time! With practice in the morning and games in the afternoon and evening, you would have thought these boys would have had enough baseball, but here they were playing hot box.

The hot-box drill the kids play on their own is usually a three-player drill with one being the runner and the other two the infielders. However, the hot-box drill I recommend in practice is a five-player drill, with each infielder having a backup who rotates into the play whenever the fielder he backs up throws the ball. Charts 5, 6, and 7 explain three versions of this drill.

CHART 5. "HOT BOX" DRILL BETWEEN FIRST AND SECOND BASES

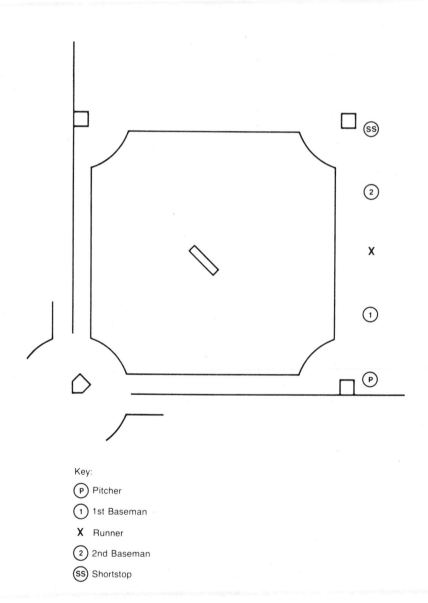

Key:

(P) Pitcher

(1) 1st Baseman

X Runner

(2) 2nd Baseman

(SS) Shortstop

CHART 6. "HOT BOX" DRILL BETWEEN SECOND AND THIRD BASES

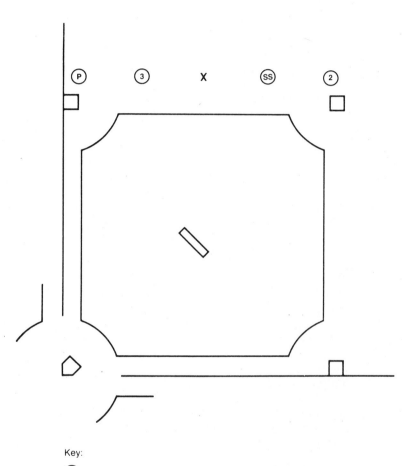

Key:

(2) 2nd Baseman

(SS) Shortstop

X Runner

(3) 3rd Baseman

(P) Pitcher

CHART 7. "HOT BOX" DRILL BETWEEN THIRD BASE AND HOME

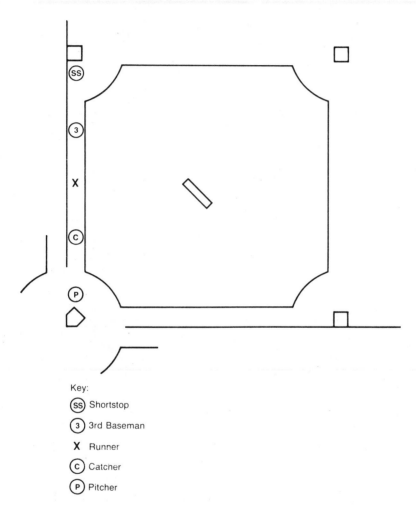

Key:

(SS) Shortstop

(3) 3rd Baseman

X Runner

(C) Catcher

(P) Pitcher

Figure 4–5 shows a hot-box situation between first and second bases, Figure 4–6 the play between second and third, and Figure 4–7 the play between third and home. In each case, as the fielder throws the ball, he moves away from the line of fire and falls in behind his former backup, who is now on the line of fire. This routine requires drilling until the fielders are able to do it smoothly and automatically.

4-5. Runner trapped in "hot box" between first and second. Pitcher, first baseman, second baseman, and shortstop are involved.

4-6. Hot-box drill between second and third involves second baseman, shortstop, third baseman, and pitcher.

4-7. Pitcher, catcher, third baseman, and shortstop try to tag out runner in hot box between third and home.

Defensively, the emphasis needs to be placed on four objectives:

1. Make as few throws as possible.
2. Chase the runner back to his previous base.
3. Fake throws to force change in direction.
4. Run him down if you can (as opposed to a throw that may go astray).

Offensively, the emphasis should be on the following:

1. Force as many throws as possible.
2. Fake direction change to force a throw.
3. Try to get to the next base.
4. Avoid the tag.

Notice in Figures 4–8 to 4–10 that the pitcher is involved in every rundown play. His importance as a contributing infielder cannot be better emphasized than in a hot-box drill.

BASE-RUNNER SIGNS

The three basic signs for a base coach are:

- windmill: keep going
- palms facing runner: stop
- palms on ground: slide

The best drill for base coaches and runners is for the coach to stand behind the third-base coach as runners come around second, heading for third. In a stage whisper, tell the base coach either "Stop," "Slide," or "Keep going," and see if the coach gives the correct sign and if the base runner executes correctly.

Players enjoy being base coaches, and I try to let the boys who play the least coach the most as compensation. You can always call time and substitute a coach if you want to send special instructions to the base runner with a more savvy coach.

The base coaches need to be drilled on the three things that they need to remind the base runner between pitches:

1. how many outs (index finger, one out; index finger and little finger, two outs)
2. whether there are other runners on base;
3. applicable rules; such as run on anything or run on a ground ball. He should be picking these up from the dugout and repeating them to the base runner.

SITUATION DRILLS

In situation drills for base running, the coach stands near the pitcher's mound, and all the players line up behind first-base to take a turn as the coach calls out the situation. For a quicker workout, have all the players line up along the first-base line, draw a line in the dirt through second base, and have them run from their spot on the first base line to the same spot on the second-base line. This drill can also be done for running from second to third and third to home.

Here is the list of the situations the coach will call out, and beside each is what the runner is expected to do.

Coach calls out situation from first base	**Runner(s) should**
1. "The pitch reaches the front of the plate."	1. Run three steps toward second.
2. "It's a ground ball."	2. Keep running to second.
3. "The catcher missed the ball."	3. Keep running to second.
4. "It's a pop-up to the infield."	4. Stop after three steps and watch to see if it is caught.
5. "The infielder misses the pop-up."	5. Run to second.
6. "It's a fly ball to the outfield."	6. Go halfway to second and watch the outfielders.

Coach calls out situation	**Runner(s) should**
7. "The outfielder catches it."	7. Return to first base.
8. "The outfielder misses it."	8. Run to second.
9. "There are runners on first and second with no outs (or one out); it's a pop-up to the infield."	9. Stay on the base (it's an infield fly).
10. "It's through the infield."	10. Think about going two bases.

From second base with runner at first

Situations 1–10 are the same as running from first.

From second base with no other runners on base

All situations except 2 and 5 are the same as running from first.

2. "It's a ground ball."	2. On a ground ball, the runner runs the three steps and stops. If the throw is to second or third he gets back; if the throw is to first he runs to third.
5. "The infielder misses the pop-up."	5. If the infielder misses the ball, he doesn't have to run.

From third base with bases loaded

All situations except 3 and 6 are the same as running from first. Situations 7, 8, and 10 are not applicable.

3. "The catcher missed the ball."	3. If the catcher misses the ball or it's a wild pitch, the runner will go if it is easy to steal home or

Coach calls out situation	Runner(s) should
	the game is tied in the last inning. (With a good catcher, the ball will have to bounce away from the catcher for there to be a good chance to steal.)
6. "It's a fly ball to the outfield."	6. On a fly ball to the outfield, the runner returns to the bag to tag up and score on a fly ball. He leaves the base as soon as the ball hits the outfielder's glove.

From third base late in the game with the score tied

1. "The pitch reaches the front of the plate."	1. The best runners can take five steps.
2. "It's a ground ball."	2. Only the fastest runner can score if the infielder throws to first.
3. "The catcher missed the ball."	3. If it is hard to steal home, the runner goes only if the ball bounces to the left or right; fast runner takes a chance.
4. "It's a pop-up to the infield."	4. Don't run.
5. "The infielder misses the pop-up."	5. Don't run.
6. "It's a fly ball to the outfield."	6. Tag up.
7. "The outfielder catches it."	7. Run home after tagging.
8. "The outfielder misses it."	8. Run home after tagging.

5
DRILLS FOR PREGAME PRACTICE

It is important that team members be physically ready to play ball—important not only in their ability to perform, but also important in avoiding injuries.

Picture this situation at our ballpark during the final innings of the first of two different games scheduled: The concession stand is lined with kids trying to buy and consume that last Coke and hot dog before their game starts. And many of them are downing the last bite as their team takes to the field.

Pregame conditioning is important, but it is also important to condition the kids and their parents to understand that the players are expected to arrive at the field at least one half hour before game time, and to spend that time in pregame conditioning, not in feeding their faces.

PREGAME CONDITIONING

Calisthenics can be made fun by letting the kids take turns leading them. They will vie for the opportunity. Five minutes of calisthenics to loosen up can consist of such standard

5-1. Jumping jacks are a good exercise to loosen arms and legs.

conditioning exercises as jumping jacks, arm exercises, and push-ups (shown in Figures 5–1, 5–2, and 5–3). The leaders call out the exercise and then call out the rhythm: "1, 2, that's 1; 1, 2, that's 2; 1, 2, that's 3"; and so on.

When the team takes the field for pregame warm-ups, usually only 15 minutes are possible, and you want infield, outfield, pitching, and batting practice squeezed into that time. Believe it or not, it can be done!

5-2. Arm stretches and arm circles are good shoulder and arm exercises.

5-3. Push-ups tune up the whole body.

You can have your starting battery (pitcher and catcher) warm up between the pitcher's mound and home plate, with a batter with bat and helmet standing in the batter's box, pretending to hit. It is the most realistic warm-up situation you can create.

Between home and third base, you can have a coach, with catcher, hitting infield and outfield balls. At the home plate area, you can have a batter hitting into the backstop and a coach tossing the ball underhand to him. With the batter and coach on opposite sides of home plate, there will be no interference between them and the pitcher and catcher warming up.

You can have another coach standing at the foul line beyond first base hitting fly balls to the outfielders.

Chart 8 shows the positioning of coaches and players in this plan of pregame drills. Chart 9 diagrams what I call the "Around the Horn" throwing drill. It can be used as a pregame drill to loosen up the arms and fine tune the accuracy of your infielders' throws. It can also be used in a regular practice drill by letting substitute fielders take a turn at each infield position, in rotation, as diagrammed.

CHART 8. PRE-GAME DRILL

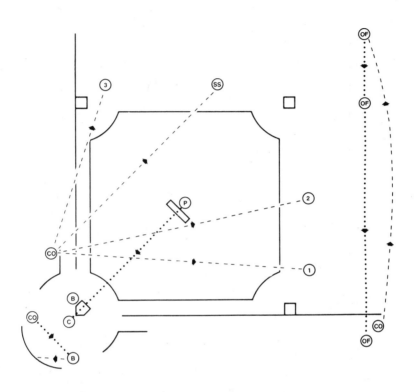

Key:
- – – – – – Batted Ball
- • • • • • • • • Thrown Ball
- (CO) Coach
- (B) Batter

CHART 9. "AROUND THE HORN" THROWING DRILL

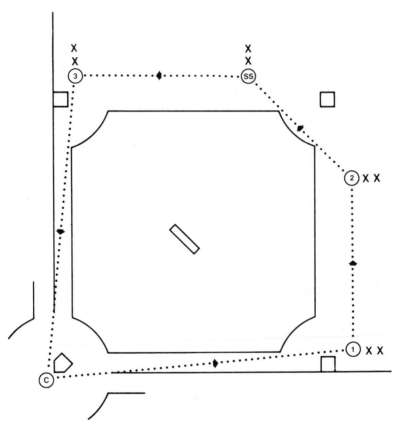

Key:

X Substitute waiting his turn

• • • • • • • Path of thrown ball

SKULL DRILL

While the other team is warming up, get your team in the dugout for a pregame "skull drill." Because of the short retention span of 9- to 12-year-olds, you can't review the basics too often. They should include the topics reviewed here.

Batting Signals

I keep batting signals simple: hit (coach claps his hands); take (coach shows the bunting position, because he wants the batter to "fake bunt" to draw a ball from the pitcher); bunt (coach touches his cap). To make the signs look complicated to confuse any would-be "sign stealers," I tell our boys the real sign is the third one. Normally, so the batter doesn't get confused, the first two signs are always the same, so he gets used to that sequence and is ready for the third sign.

Where to Stand in the Batter's Box

If the opposing pitcher has a strong fast-ball, I remind the players to stand as far back in the batter's box as possible to give them maximum time to watch the pitch. Conversely, if he is a "junk pitcher," I tell them to stand forward in the batter's box so they can hit the ball in front of the plate before it arches down.

Base-Running Signs

A review of base-running signs is for the benefit of base runners and base coaches (who must be players). Again, the signs are simple: slide (hands close to the ground); stop, standing up (hands at chest in stop signal); keep going (windmill with right arm). The most frequently forgotten base-coaching assignment is that of the on-deck batter, who should stand in a position where he can be seen by the runner coming from third to home.

Base-Running Rules

I review three rules of base running:

1. With two outs, run on anything.
2. With less than two outs, tag up on a fly ball.
3. In a force play situation, run on a ground ball.

Pitching/Catching Rules

I cover four rules for pitching and catching:

1. Keep the ball low on the good hitters.
2. Throw from the stretch position to the weak hitters if you are having control problems.
3. Catcher must give the pitcher a good target, adjusting it to compensate. For example, give an inside target if the pitcher is consistently throwing outside.
4. Pitcher must cover home with a runner on third in a wild pitch–passed ball situation.

I have a checklist of these coaching tips that I pull out of my pocket for the pregame skull session. The boys expect it and can almost recite it. When they *can* recite it, I know they will have a good chance of remembering the coaching tips in game situations.

The manager of the Little League All-Star team from Taiwan was quoted in *USA Today* as saying, before his team entered the 1986 Little League World Series, "In school our children are taught to learn through repetitive exercise. We apply the same philosophy in baseball through drilling in the fundamentals." It obviously is a success formula, for the Taiwanese Little Leaguers have won 10 Little League World Series titles.

In working with children of Little League age, repetition is the only way you can hope to have a youngster perform the way he should in a game situation. This means repetition in batting, fielding, base-running, and pitching drills, and also repetition in the important skull session part of baseball.

6

STRATEGY FOR DEALING WITH PARENTS

In the *Chicago Tribune* review of my first book, *Managing Little League Baseball*, Robert Cross started his article by saying, "Little League when used as a modifier for the word 'parent,' has become, in some circles, a synonym for abusive, overbearing, insensitive, or warped." Ironically, last year, my final year as a Little League manager, I had *more* problems with disgruntled parents than in previous years. After 20 years, you would think I would be used to it, but I wasn't, and the biased criticism still hurt.

In one instance, a father unceremoniously turned in his son's uniform after a game in which his son had played only three innings, because his son "would never make the All-Star team if that's all he gets to play!" Another father announced he was pulling his son off the team because one of our coaches had criticized his son for making two errors. In another incident, involving a parent who wasn't interested enough to bring her son to practice or games, I replaced her son with a Minor League player after her son missed two consecutive games without reason (which is our league rule).

The boy's mother made a scene at the next game, saying if we were *really* interested in her son, we would have arranged for transportation for him when it wasn't convenient for her or her husband to bring him. The final disappointing confrontation was with a father and good friend who thought his son should have been nominated for the All-Star team, even though the two coaches and I were unanimous in not nominating him.

Disappointing? Of course! Rare? Unfortunately not, because any Little League manager or coach who has been involved in Little League very long can match these with his own redneck-parent stories. In a large city newspaper near here last summer, there was a running controversy in the Letters to the Editor column that continued for two weeks, started by an irate Little League mother whose boy was chosen for the All-Star team, but then rode the bench. She accused the manager of playing, in place of her son, his own son, who in her opinion was not as good as hers.

It pointed up the annual problem with All-Star teams and All-Star parents: Every boy on the 14-team roster was a star of his local team during the regular season and probably played in all 6 innings of every game. Now, however, he is one of 14 All-Stars, with only 9 positions on the team. What usually results in close All-Star games is that the 9 starters, who in the manager's judgment are his best players, play the entire game, and the other 5 All-Stars warm the bench. That situation is *guaranteed* to upset 5 All-Star parents.

How do you tell a father who criticizes you for not playing his son more so he can make the All-Star team, that his son couldn't make the All-Star team if he played every inning of every game? How do you tell a parent whose child is criticized for making errors that coaching is not just praising kids for doing well? How do you tell a mother that you *are* interested in her child, but not to the extent of providing a taxi service to and from practice and games? And how do you explain to a father who had *his* heart set on his boy's making the All-Star team that, in the unbiased opinion of a manager and two coaches, his son just wasn't good enough?

When a father yanks his child off your team in anger, it is tempting to tell him where he and his child can go. All that does, however, is penalize the child, *who really wants to play if his dad just wouldn't interfere.* With the two incidents mentioned where the fathers pulled their boys off the team, I let the situation cool for a day and then talked to the fathers. In both cases, by that time, they realized they were only hurting their boys. As a face-saving step for them, I suggested each let his son decide whether he wanted to continue to play. Each agreed, and predictably the son was ready, willing, and anxious to rejoin the team.

With respect to the mother who thought I should provide taxi service for her son, I would not compromise. I told her the coaches and I spent enough hours at the field working with her son, and she should do her part in getting him there and home. I had given them one warning that we had an obligation to bring up a Minor League boy if her son continued to miss practice and games, and when she ignored the warning, we replaced her son with a boy who was eager to play and whose parents were willing to do their part.

The problems with abusive parents have been cyclical in our league. We will go for several years without any serious problems and then have a raft of controversies the next year.

The attitude of the league in supporting its managers, coaches, and umpires is key to keeping the situation under control. It is highly desirable to have a majority of board members unaffiliated with any team so that objectivity is possible when a controversy occurs. And it is important that situations that can create controversies are avoided. A crucial game this past season, which was a makeup of a rainout, was played on a Saturday evening when getting umpires became a problem. The president of our league agreed to supply the umpires and advised us who they were. I pointed out that one of the men, although a good umpire, had a son on the opposing team, and I thought it was unwise to put him in that situation. My objection was overruled, and the father/umpire was allowed to umpire behind the plate. I think he would have done a good job if the parents and manager of his son's team had left him alone. They so intimidated him that he lost control of the game, which was fraught with controversies. It was an assignment that never should have been allowed.

We must be conscious that a new generation of parents is moving up to Little League each year, along with their sons, while the more seasoned parents have moved up to Senior League. Unless good attitudes and parent control have been established in your Minor Leagues, that influx of one-third new redneck parents could be enough to upset the stability of last year's good crop of parents. As I mentioned in my earlier book, the younger the player, the more protective his parents are, and the more likely to overreact when their child is called out on strikes, is criticized by his coach, or breaks into tears for any number of reasons that are dictated by the pressure of his first serious encounter with competitive sports.

And as I recommended in *Managing Little League Baseball*, the more communications a manager establishes with his team's parents, the less likely will be misunderstandings and confrontations between parent and coach.

Mike Powers agrees with the need for communications between managers/coaches and parents. In Figure 6–1 is a copy of the letter he sends to the parents of his players. It is interesting to note in the third paragraph that he says to the parents ". . . and I will leave it to you to develop the parent organization that St. Matthews Little League expects us to have. (I will have descriptions for each of these parent positions with me at practice . . .)."

So many managers think that they have to carry the whole burden of the team. Mike makes it clear that he expects the parents to assume part of the responsibility. It then becomes an adult team effort running parallel with their children's team effort on the field.

In Mike's league in St. Matthews, Kentucky, the Board of Directors sends a questionnaire to all parents, asking them to evaluate the league and give their recommendations. It even asks them to evaluate their son's manager and coach. I found the questions indicative of the league's goals of sportsmanship, skills, enthusiasm, and so forth. The absence of emphasis on won-lost record puts that in its proper perspective (Figure 6–2).

FIGURE 6-1

FIRST NATIONAL BANK TEAM

March 24, 1986

Dear First National Parents,

Jon and I are very pleased to have your sons on the team. We will try our best to do all the right things for the team and your children. We will teach them good sportsmanship, how to work together as a team, and how to work to improve. We will also be as objective as we can in determining who will play each position and where they will bat in the batting order.

Practices will be held at St. Albert's field at 5:45 P.M. Monday through Thursday for the first two weeks (March 24–April 3), with a scrimmage game being planned for Saturday, March 29. Then we will *not* have practice during the school spring break, but will resume on Monday, April 14, at 5:45 P.M., and practice Monday through Thursday of that week. If it rains during practices, we'll move to my garage for a skull session (1810 Girard). The first game and the parade will be on April 19.

On April 3, we will have a parents' meeting at the field after practice to assure that we have volunteers for all the parent positions: business manager, player agent, picnic chairman, etc. We have all been through this several times before, and I will leave it to you to develop the parent organization that St. Matthews Little League expects us to have. (I will have descriptions for each of these parent positions with me at practice if you would like copies.)

Also, if anyone who has a VCR camera would be willing to film some during practices or games, please talk with us.

If you have any questions or suggestions, let us know.

Sincerely,

Mike Powers
Manager
Jon Mindrum
Coach

1986 Roster   St. Matthews Little League Baseball, Inc.   Team Name First National

PLAYERS	AGE	BIRTHDATE	JERSEY NO.	PARENTS	ADDRESS	ZIP	PHONE
Michael Bailey	11	10/1/74		Ron/Sharon	212 Blankenbaker	40207	555-5000
Brian Clarke	12	4/1/74		Lloyd/Janet	224 Bramton Rd.	40207	555-0494
Scott Herman	12	10/25/73		Jan	1303 Ambridge Dr.	40207	555-6072
Jason Hawkins	12	1/16/74		Dennis/Sheryl	180 Vernon	40206	555-6340
Grayson Abell	11	6/24/75		Darnell	1010 Ambridge Dr.	40207	555-4655
Michael Mindrum	11	12/2/74		Jen/Janet	2319 Stoneleigh Ct.	40222	555-6288
Tom Powers	11	4/18/75		Mike/Kathy	1810 Girard Dr.	40222	555-0497
Chad Guelda	11	12/4/74		Charles/Maryle	4734 Brownsboro Rd.	40207	555-5590
Scott Scholtz	10	8/13/75		Jan Reis/Dawn	6303 Glenn Hill Rd.	40222	555-8090
Doug Abell	10	10/8/75		Doug/Rose	1004 Weymouth Ct.	40222	555-0856
Sam Graham	10	10/31/75		Kyle/Kathy	4802 Bilander Rd.	40222	555-0383
Stephen Webb	11	2/2/75		Bob/Patricia	7800 Pine Meadows	40222	555-2660

Manager Mike Powers   Phone 555-0497   Days Mon.–Thurs.   Times 5:45 P.M.

Coach John Mindrum   Phone 555-6288   Locations St. Alberts

Business Mgr. _____ Phone _____   Parents Auxillary Rep. _____ Phone _____

Scorekeeper _____ Phone _____   Telephone Chrm. _____ Phone _____

_____ Phone _____   Team Picnic Chrm. _____

Concession Stand Tele. # _____

FIGURE 6-2

Dear parents,

Your child's participation in St. Matthews Little League Baseball is intended to be a beneficial and positive experience. The objective is to provide a healthful activity while promoting an appreciation for good sportsmanship, teamwork, and discipline.

To assist us in assuring this goal is achieved, we would appreciate your thoughts, observations, and comments in completing the questionnaire on the reverse side. Hopefully, your input will enable us to maintain, or improve, the fine program we have at St. Matthews.

While we ask that you include your name, address, and phone number, it is not a requirement. Please return your completed questionnaire to the concession stand before you leave the park today.

Thank you for taking the time to assist us.

Board of Directors
St. Matthews Little League Baseball, Inc.

ST. MATTHEWS LITTLE LEAGUE BASEBALL
PROGRAM EVALUATION QUESTIONNAIRE

Team _____

Please circle the number that expresses your impressions of the Little League program. Five (5) indicates strong agreement; three (3), neutral; one (1), strong disagreement. If you are in strong disagreement with any question, please provide us with your thoughts in the Comments section.

1. The program teaches the importance of good sportsmanship.   5 4 3 2 1

2. Your child enjoyed and looked forward to practice.   5 4 3 2 1

3. Your child enjoyed and looked forward to the games.   5 4 3 2 1

4. You feel your child improved his/her skills during the season.   5 4 3 2 1

5. How do you evaluate the program's equipment?   5 4 3 2 1

6. How do you evaluate the program's facilities?   5 4 3 2 1

7. Your child's manager/coach was enthusiastic/positive during games and practices.   5 4 3 2 1

8. Please evaluate the manager's/coach's effectiveness during games and practices in regard to:

   Teaching skills   5 4 3 2 1

   Individual attention   5 4 3 2 1

   Gaining your child's attention   5 4 3 2 1

9. Please provide your overall rating of: The team manager   5 4 3 2 1
         The team coach   5 4 3 2 1

10. You are interested in your child participating in next year's baseball program.   5 4 3 2 1

11. The St. Matthews Little League program met your expectations.   5 4 3 2 1

12. Please rate the overall St. Matthews Little League program.   5 4 3 2 1

COMMENTS: Please provide us with your thoughts regarding any problems you feel exist or any suggestions you have. _____

_____

If you are interested in participating in the operation of the St. Matthews Little League program, please indicate your area of interest: ☐ Team Manager* ☐ Team Coach* ☐ Scorekeeper* ☐ Umpire* ☐ Board Member*
               *Indicate major, minor or t-ball division

OPTIONAL: Parent's Name (please print) _____ Child's Name _____

        Address _____

        Phone _____ Team _____

7

STRATEGY FOR TRAINING UMPIRES, MANAGERS, AND COACHES

A recent conversation among a group of our managers touched on the caliber of the umpiring during the preceding week in our league. Each manager had his story about the one the umpires missed, and naturally the managers whose teams lost were the most critical of the umpiring.

To play the devil's advocate, I asked them if they had ever seen an umpire change a judgment call. They all admitted they had not, but in the discussion it became clear that not all of them really understood the difference between a judgment call and a rule call. For the reader who may also be unclear about the distinction, examples of judgment calls are:

- balls and strikes
- out or safe
- leaving base too soon

Examples of rule calls are:

- batting out of order
- infield fly rule (although judgment can be a factor in

determining position of ball and reasonable effort
needed to catch it)
- balks (judgment can also be a factor in calling some
balks)

It is clear that judgment calls are more frequent, and even
some rule calls are affected by judgment. And there is no
doubt that most disputes are over the judgment calls of balls
and strikes and decisions of out or safe at the bases (see
Figure 7-1).

To further bait my fellow managers, I asked why they
wasted the time, energy, and frustration over a judgment call
when they all admitted they had never seen an umpire reverse
himself on one. They were stuck for an answer until one of
them finally said, "To keep him honest." I'll buy that reason
if it was a case where the umpire obviously blew one, and you
want to let him know you know it, because he may let the
next close one go your way.

A celebrated case in point occurred in professional sports
during the fifth playoff game for the NBA Championship in
1986 between the Boston Celtics and the Houston Rockets.
The Celtics were leading in the best of seven games series,
three games to one, so this was a do or die game for the

7-1. Umpire in proper position to make judgment call of out
at first base.

Rockets. Suddenly a fight erupted, and the Rockets' hopes were apparently dashed when their star center Ralph Sampson was thrown out of the game. There was much speculation on whether, in such a crucial game, the referee used good judgment in imposing such a severe penalty. *It was a judgment call.* But the Rockets won the game without Sampson, and then there was much speculation on whether the referees called the close ones in the Rockets' favor during the rest of the game to compensate for a bad call against the Rockets earlier. Who knows? But it certainly is possible, since professional basketball officials, just like volunteer baseball umpires, are human.

EFFECTS OF CALLS

The point is that an umpire's alleged bad call will seldom *directly* affect the outcome of a game, but it is possible that it could *indirectly* affect it in several ways. In the Celtics-Rockets game, the judgment call to eject Sampson could have *indirectly* affected the outcome by prompting later overcompensating calls against the Celtics; or it could have *indirectly* affected the outcome by motivating the rest of the Rockets to play "over their heads" to compensate for Sampson's loss. Or it could have been a combination of the two factors.

In 20 years of Little League experience, I have seen few instances in which an umpire's judgment call has directly affected the outcome of a game. Those few instances have been situations such as two outs, bottom of the sixth, and the tying run on third trying to score. The umpire must make a safe/out judgment call on a close play, and the manager whose team gets the wrong call will argue that he lost the game on the umpire's call, forgetting the many other crucial plays during the game that affected the outcome, in which the umpire may not have even been a factor.

More vivid in my 20-year Little League memory have been the cases where an umpire's call has had an *indirect* effect on a game. The most frequent cases have been those in which a player allowed an umpire's call to affect him *mentally* so badly that he could not perform well *physically* after the call. Such situations arise when the pitcher blows up over an umpire's ball/strike call and completely loses his pitching effectiveness, or a batter is so affected on a third-strike call that he is still thinking about it when he blows an easy ground ball in the defensive half of the inning. And on his next time at bat he's practically a basket case.

The high-strung, uptight Little Leaguer is most susceptible, and some of the best players are either naturally that way or parent-pressured that way. They will lose their cool over an umpire's close call that doesn't go their way, which may not have *any* effect on the game, but because they lost their cool they are unable to regain it again throughout the rest of the game. Subconsciously it may even be an escape valve from the pressure—if they don't do well during the rest of the game, it was all the umpire's fault. That kind of attitude on their parents' part helps contribute to the parent problems covered in Chapter 6.

INVISIBLE UMPIRES

What's the answer? I preach the philosophy that the umpires are invisible. They aren't even there; they are programmed robots that sometimes call them your way and sometimes the other way. They are lights on the scoreboard that tell you the balls and strikes and outs. Forget they exist!

We reinforce that philosophy every time a batter looks to the bench for sympathy on a called strike, comes back to the dugout after being called out on a close base play, or looks to the dugout from the pitcher's mound after a ball that he thought should been called a strike. We just say, "The umpire's invisible!" and they get the message.

As any coach will tell you, so much in sports is mental. A Little League coach must mentally as well as physically condition his players how to play and how to accept disappointment as well as victory.

In my business career in sales and marketing, I sometimes hear our inside administrative staff complain about our customers being wrong. There is an old sales cliché, "The customer is always right," which I like to amend by saying "The customer is always right, even when he's wrong!" The analogy applies to umpires as well: The umpire is always right, *even when he's wrong!*

You need to press that point to your players by getting them to *believe* that umpires are invisible; that they call as many close ones for you as against you; that they just call 'em as they see 'em. To the player who persists in criticizing the umpire's calls, you may need to get even tougher and threaten to bench him if he doesn't follow your coaching. I did that with one boy, and his father was understanding enough to tell me later it was the best thing that could have happened to his son, because we never had the problem with him again.

Will umpires ever deliberately cheat? In my experience, the only umpires whose integrity could be questioned are those umpires who are dragged out of the stands and asked to "volunteer." Invariably they are the fathers of the boys on one competing team or the other. They don't know the rules; and even if they do, they will have an obvious bias when calling a close play.

PRESEASON ORGANIZING

In *Managing Little League*, we emphasized the importance of organizing preseason training meetings of managers, coaches, and umpires (in the same meetings). We required every Senior League and Little League team to provide an umpire for the opposite league, and we then recruited other adults to fill out the assigned three-member crews. We also published a list of alternates and gave each umpire the responsibility of calling an alternate to take his place if he couldn't make an assignment. We do not pay our umpires, and we schedule them for only one evening per week (a doubleheader for the Little League umpires and a single game for the Senior League umpires). That is certainly not asking too much of any umpire.

A number of our coaches and managers umpire in the

opposite league, so it does require a scheduling job to make sure they are not assigned to umpire on a night when their team plays. We also have to schedule around dads so they aren't scheduled to umpire their kids' games.

One thing we have added to our training for umpires and coaches, since *Managing Little League* was published, is a "final exam," which we have reproduced at the end of this chapter. Anyone who scores 100 percent is well qualified to coach or umpire, with respect to understanding the basic rules. We have included an answer key to the exam, and have noted the rule that applies to each question. If you are uncertain about an answer, a review of the appropriate rule will supply it. Please check, because there are several trick questions.

SKULL SESSIONS

You can't expect to have a good rapport between managers, coaches, and umpires unless you develop it. Just as I recommend skull sessions between coaches and players on your team, I recommend skull sessions between managers, coaches, and umpires in your league.

Attached as Figure 7–2 is the training program outline for our skull sessions with managers, coaches, and umpires. We augment it by having an experienced umpire teach umpire field positions. We have tried one, two, and three meetings and found that one is too few and three is too many. The Saturday before our season opens, we have a day of practice games, with every team playing and every umpire crew working. And just as managers are observing and coaching their players, we have umpire coaches observing and constructively coaching the umpires.

We assign three umpires to a crew and appoint crew chiefs from among our more experienced, more dependable umpires. We didn't use to do that, but found that the title of crew chief gave that umpire an extra responsibility that he took to heart. Rarely did a crew chief not show up, and often he would get on members of his crew who were late or failed to

FIGURE 7-2

Summersville Little League
Training Program Outline

A. GENERAL INFORMATION

   1. Ages of players.
   2. Number of players per team.
   3. Number of players per age level.
   4. Dates of player drafts.
   5. Dates of player cuts.
   6. Roster deadlines.
   7. Opening day.
   8. Adding players to fill vacancies.

B. LOCAL LEAGUE RULES

   1. Starting times of games.
   2. Rainout schedule.
   3. Substitutions (see Reg. IV [i], page 13; rules 3.03, 3.05, 3.06, 3.07, and 3.08, page 29).
   4. Mercy rule.
   5. Managers, Coaches, and Spectator Control (see Reg. XIV, page 16; rules 4.06 and 4.07, page 31).

C. KEY RESPONSIBILITIES OF UMPIRES

   1. Authority (Rule 9.01, page 47).
   2. Judgment call final (Rule 9.02 [a], page 47).
   3. Manager may appeal rule interpretation (Rule 9.02 [b] and [c], page 47.
   4. Conflicting decisions on same play by two umpires (Rule 9.04 [c], page 48).
   5. Deciding fitness of field (Rules 3.10 and 4.01 [d], page 30).
   6. Starting game (Rule 4.01, page 30).
   7. Called games and tie games (Rules 4.10 and 4.11, page 32; Rule 4.12, page 33; examples on page 62).
   8. Forfeited games (rules 4.15, 4.16, 4.17, and 4.18, page 33).
   9. Protested games (Rule 4.19, pages 33 and 34).
  10. Live and dead ball (Rule 5.02, page 34; Rules 5.08, 5.09, 5.10, 5.11, page 35).
  11. Umpires hand signs ("The Right Call," pages 5, 10, 22, 25, 31, 35, 37, 41, 43).
  12. Base umpires' field positions ("Umpire in Little League," pages 9-26).

D. KEY RULES REGARDING THE BATTER

    1. When pitcher ready (Rule 6.02 [b], page 36).
    2. Both feet in batter's box (Rule 6.03, page 36).
    3. Batter out (Rule 6.05, page 36; and Rule 6.06, page 37).
    4. Batting out of turn (Rule 6.07, pages 37 and 38).
    5. Hit by pitched ball (Rule 6.08 [b], page 38).
    6. Foul ball (Definition, page 25).
    7. Foul tip (Definition, page 26).
    8. Infield fly rule (Definition, page 26; Rule 7.08 [f], page 41; Rule 6.05 [e] and [l], page 36).
    9. Strike and strike zone (Definitions, page 27).
   10. Hitting pitch on the bounce (Definitions—"In flight," page 26).
   11. Intentional walk (Rule 4.03 [a], page 31).
   12. Catch (Definition, page 24).
   13. Protective equipment (rules 1.16 and 1.17, page 24).

E. KEY RULES REGARDING THE RUNNER

    1. Two runners on same base (Rule 7.03, page 39).
    2. Glove thrown at batted ball (Rule 7.05 [b], page 40).
    3. Glove thrown at thrown ball (Rule 7.05 [d], page 40).
    4. Ground-rule double (Rule 7.05 [f], page 40).
    5. Ground-rule wild throw (Rule 7.05 [g], page 40).
    6. Wild pitch out of play (Rule 7.05 [b], page 40).
    7. Obstruction (Definition, page 27; Rule 7.06, page 40).
    8. Interference (Definition, page 26; Rule 7.08 [b], page 41; Rule 7.09, page 42; Rule 7.11, page 43; Rule 3.16, page 30).
    9. Passing preceding runner (Rule 7.08 [b], page 41).
   10. Overrunning first base (Rule 7.08 [j], page 41).
   11. Appeals (Definition, page 24; Rule 7.10, page 42; Rule 4.09 [a] and [b], pages 31 and 32; Rule 6.07 [a] and [b], page 37; Rule 7.06 [d], page 41.
   12. Leaving base too soon (Rule 7.13, pages 43 and 44; "Umpire in Little League," pages 6 and 7).
   13. No courtesy runners (Rule 3.04, page 29).
   14. Tag (Definition, page 28).
   15. Running out of base line (Rule 7.08 [a], page 40).
   16   Runner to first interfering with throw (Rule 7.09 [b], page 42).

F. KEY RULES REGARDING THE PITCHER

    1. Maximum pitching time per week (Reg. IV, page 13).

 2. Mandatory rest between pitching assignments (Reg. VI, pages 13 and 14).
 3. Age limitations (Reg. VI, page 14).
 4. Pitcher removed (Reg. VI, page 14).
 5. Legal pitching positions (Rule 8.01, pages 44 and 45).
 6. Preparatory pitches (Rule 8.03, pages 44 and 45).
 7. Balks (Rule 8.05, page 46).
 8. Illegal pitch (Definition, page 26).
 9. Visits by manager or coach (Rule 8.06, page 46).

get a substitute when unable to serve. It was not unusual to have only two out of three assigned umpires show; last-minute work or personal problems do occur. But it was extremely rare to have only one show, and we never had no members of an assigned crew show.

Attached as Figure 7–3 is our schedule for the 1986 season, listing all the names and phone numbers of team managers, umpires, and alternate umpires, in addition, of course, to the league schedule and umpiring assignments. Local rules were also attached in order to provide in one packet everything a manager, coach, or umpire needed for communications. We made enough copies available for every manager, coach, and umpire in the league, and put each individual's name on a set, so those who missed the meeting when they were passed out would be sure to get their set at the next opportunity. We had extra copies at the refreshment stand and posted the sheets, page by page, on our bulletin board.

FIGURE 7-3

TO: Little League umpires and managers
FROM: Ned McIntosh, Umpire-in-Chief
DATE: April 8, 1986
RE: Umpiring schedule and procedures

Attached are the team and umpiring schedules for 1986. Please mark your calendar for the days you play and/or umpire. Note the following procedures:

(1) Schedule Conflicts
I have avoided all conflicts with the game schedules of those umpires who coach or play for another team. If you find you have a personal conflict with any assigned dates, please take the responsibility of obtaining your own replacement. Trade dates with another umpire, call one of the umpires on alternate list (all umpires' names and phone numbers are attached), call your crew chief, or call me; but don't just fail to show, since you may cause the delay or postponement of a game.

(2) Equipment
Please wear dark trousers to complete your uniforms, and always be in complete uniform to add professionalism to your position. Game balls should be obtained at the concession stand, and equipment is in the scorekeeper's room. Please return all equipment after the game.

(3) Postponed Games
It is the responsibility of the home team manager to notify the umpires if a game will be postponed for any reason. Otherwise, teams and umpires should report to the field and the question of whether a game should start or not will be decided in accordance with the rules. Please decide then, with teams and umpires present, when the game will be rescheduled. (See chart indicating when game should be rescheduled in the attached local rules.)

Umpires who have a schedule conflict with the rescheduled date should take the responsibility of getting a replacement, but if managers make last-minute schedule changes, then the home team manager must be responsible for obtaining the umpires.
Names and phone numbers of umpires, alternate umpires, and

home team managers are attached for your use in communicating with each other.

Thanks for your cooperation and service to our youngsters. If you have any questions, feel free to call me at home (555-4651) or at work (555-3000).

Summersville Little League, 1986

Team	Managers	Phone
Pirates	Brooks Groves	555-3230
Yankees	Bill Cook	555-4356
Giants	Ned McIntosh	555-4651
Reds	Sonny Talbert	555-3041
A's (Birch River)	Bobby Mullens	555-4641
Cardinals	Jim Fitzwater	555-2292
Padres	Dave Keenan	555-5257
Phillies	Cotton Snuffer	555-1079
Expos	Delmar Tate	555-1225
Cubs	Dave Whitlock	555-2886

Umpire Crews

Crew A		Crew D	
John D. McClung*	555-1248	Buell Moses*	555-4393
Jeff Girod	555-3422	Lee Tate	555-1225
T. Tom Cook	555-3137	Bobby White	555-3399

Crew B		Crew E	
Bob Hennessey*	555-6466	Steve Ramsey*	555-2257
Arthur Corbett	555-4938	Dennis Childress	555-4736
Sam Argento	555-4540	Mike Burke	555-5823

Crew C		Alternates	
Joe Whitlock*	555-4107	Stan Smith	555-3472
Stan Smith	555-3472	Dennis Childress	555-4736
Bob Hughes	555-2041	Floyd Friend	555-5390
		Tom McGirl	555-6419

*Crew Chief—responsible for assigning umpire positions.

1986 Summersville Little League Schedule

Team Numbers

1	Yankees	6	Padres
2	Reds	7	Phillies
3	Pirates	8	Cubs
4	Giants	9	Cards
5	A's	10	Expos

Practice Saturday, April 12

10:00 A.M.	2	vs.	6	Umpire Crew A
12:00 noon	1		7	Umpire Crew C
2:00 P.M.	5		8	Umpire Crew E
4:00 P.M.	3		9	Umpire Crew D
6:00 P.M.	4		10	Umpire Crew B

(first team listed is home team)

Opening Day, Saturday, April 19 (Rain Date: 4/26)

10:30 A.M.	1	vs.	6	Umpire Crew B
12:30 P.M.	2		7	Umpire Crew D
2:00 P.M.	3		8	Umpire Crew A
3:30 P.M.	4		9	Umpire Crew C
5:00 P.M.	5		10	Umpire Crew E

First Half

Day	Date	Time	H	V	Umpire Crew	Day	Date	Time	H	V	Umpire Crew
M	4/21	5:30	1	3	A	M	5/5	5:30	1	5	B
		7:30	2	4	A			7:30	2	6	B
T	4/22	5:30	5	7	B	T	5/6	5:30	3	7	A
		7:30	6	8	B			7:30	4	8	A
W	4/23	5:30	10	2	D	W	5/7	5:30	6	10	D
		7:30	9	1	D			7:30	5	9	D
Th	4/24	5:30	4	6	C	Th	5/8	5:30	8	2	C
		7:30	3	5	C			7:30	7	1	C
F	4/25	5:30	7	9	E	F	5/9	5:30	10	4	E
		7:30	8	10	E			7:30	9	3	E
M	4/28	5:30	1	4	C	M	5/12	5:30	3	4	D
		7:30	5	8	C			7:30	1	2	D
T	4/29	5:30	3	6	B	T	5/13	5:30	5	6	B
		7:30	7	10	B			7:30	9	10	B
W	4/30	5:30	8	1	A	W	5/14	5:30	7	8	A
		7:30	9	2	A			7:30	2	3	A
Th	5/1	5:30	10	3	E	Th	5/15	5:30	10	1	E
		7:30	4	7	E			7:30	4	5	E
F	5/2	5:30	2	5	D	F	5/16	5:30	8	9	C
		7:30	6	9	D			7:30	6	7	C

Second Half

Day	Date	Time	H	V	Umpire Crew
M	5/19	5:30	3	1	D
		7:30	4	2	D
T	5/20	5:30	8	6	A
		7:30	7	5	A
W	5/21	5:30	2	10	B
		7:30	1	9	B
Th	5/22	5:30	6	4	C
		7:30	5	3	C
F	5/23	5:30	10	8	E
		7:30	9	7	E
M	5/26	5:30	8	5	A
		7:30	4	1	A
T	5/27	5:30	6	3	B
		7:30	10	7	B
W	5/28	5:30	2	9	E
		7:30	1	8	E
Th	5/29	5:30	7	4	D
		7:30	3	10	D
F	5/30	5:30	5	2	C
		7:30	9	6	C

Day	Date	Time	H	V	Umpire Crew
M	6/2	5:30	6	2	B
		7:30	5	1	B
T	6/3	5:30	7	3	C
		7:30	8	4	C
W	6/4	5:30	9	5	A
		7:30	10	6	A
Th	6/5	5:30	2	8	E
		7:30	1	7	E
F	6/6	5:30	3	9	D
		7:30	4	10	D
M	6/9	5:30	2	1	A
		7:30	4	3	A
T	6/10	5:30	6	5	D
		7:30	8	7	D
W	6/11	5:30	10	9	C
		7:30	3	2	C
Th	6/12	5:30	5	4	B
		7:30	7	6	B
F	6/13	5:30	9	8	E
		7:30	1	10	E
M	6/16	5:30	7	2	A
		7:30	6	1	A
T	6/17	5:30	9	4	B
		7:30	8	3	B
W	6/18	5:30	10	5	C

Local Little League Rules, 1986

1. First Little League game starts at 5:30 P.M. No new inning should start after 7:15 P.M. (Exception: A tie game should be allowed to continue until finished.)
2. Second Little League game starts at 7:30 P.M. No new inning should start after 9:30 P.M. (Exception: On Fridays and Saturdays and after school is out.)
3. Rainouts *must* be played as follows:

> First rainout of week: Saturday, 10:00 A.M.
> Second rainout of week: Saturday, 12:00 noon
> Third rainout of week: Saturday, 1:30 P.M.
> Fourth rainout of week: Saturday, 3:00 P.M.
> Fifth rainout of week: Saturday, 4:30 P.M.
> Sixth rainout of week: Saturday, 6:00 P.M.
> Seventh rainout of week: Saturday, 7:30 P.M.

Rainouts not able to be played on Saturday should be scheduled on Sunday:

> First rainout of week: Sunday, 2:00 P.M.
> Second rainout of week: Sunday, 3:30 P.M.
> Third rainout of week: Sunday, 5:00 P.M.
> Fourth rainout of week: Sunday, 7:30 P.M.

4. Umpire crew of a rained-out game should handle the rain date. Home team manager is responsible for notifying umpires or scheduling other umpires if original crew cannot serve.
5. In Little League games, all substitutes must have entered the game by no later than the defensive half of the fourth inning.
6. Mercy Rule: If at the end of the fourth or fifth inning one team is leading by 10 or more runs, the umpire shall end the game.
7. Manager and Spectator Control

Team manager is responsible for keeping himself, his team, and his spectators under control.

If abuse of umpires and/or team members occurs, umpire will ask manager to join him in warning the party that:

(1) He will be asked to leave the park if abuse continues;
(2) If he refuses to leave the park, the player he is supporting will be suspended and both will be asked to leave the park; and
(3) In extreme cases, the game may be forfeited to the other team.

Managers and coaches must remain in the dugout at all times, except with the umpire's permission.

If a team manager or coach sets such a poor example that he is ejected from a game by an umpire, the incident should be reported by the umpire immediately after the game to the League president, who will determine if further disciplinary action is warranted.

Naturally, rule books were also provided to every manager, coach, and umpire, and extra copies were kept at the refreshment stands. We provided umpires with uniforms—cap, shirt, and jacket—and insisted they wear them to add professionalism to their appearance. We provided each umpire a counter and had extra counters at the refreshment stand. In the first training meeting, we asked all experienced umpires to search their jackets and drawers at home and bring in all of their excess counters. You would be surprised what a collection some had accumulated!

Mike Powers adds scorekeeping to the preseason training program in his league, requiring each team to assign an official scorekeeper and send him to the scorekeeper's training meeting. Figure 7–4 gives the scorekeeping training material that the St. Matthews Little League uses in its training.

Now, if you think you know Little League rules and would make a good umpire, take the Little League Baseball Quiz (Figure 7–5). The applicable rules appear in brackets after the questions, but if you still have doubts about the correct answer, check the answer key that follows.

FIGURE 7–4

St. Matthews Little League Baseball Inc.,
Scorekeeping

1. Home team keeps score; visitors announce the game.
2. Announcer controls the scoreboard.
3. Announcer:

    A. If the teams have not taken their pregame warm-up, please announce: "Will the home team take the field for warm-up" or "Will the visiting team please take the field for warm-up." Each team is given 10 minutes for warm-up.

B. Announce the rosters with the player's jersey number and position.

C. Announce the first three batters at the beginning of each team's turn at bat.

D. Announce the players' names as they come into the batter's box and on deck: "The next batter is Joe Smith and Tom Doe on deck."

E. Announce the official starting time of the game after the first pitch.

F. After each half-inning, announce the team's hits, runs, and men left on base: "So-and-so team had 3 runs on 4 hits with 2 men left on base. The score is So-and-so team 5, Do-si-do team 3."

G. At the end of the game, announce that the home team is to bring in the flag and the bases (and in the minor league, the pitching machine).

4. Scorekeepers:

A. Please use the book marked August League.

B. Mark all plays and substitutions in the scorebook.

C. It is a good idea to bring an extra sheet of paper to jot down the substitutions, then record them in the scorebook.

D. Every player will have a slot in the scorebook for the August League scorebook. The August League uses the round-robin method of batting in both leagues.

E. Record at the bottom of the page the hits, runs, and errors.

F. If unsure on how to score a play, try to jot it down on the piece of paper longhand and then refer to notes later and score it in the book.

G. Use the position numbers for each player, not the abbreviation for the position: pitcher is 1, not P.

H. Record the pitchers of the game and innings pitched in the pitcher log.

5. Announcers and scorekeepers are to be at the ballpark at least 20 to 30 minutes before the game.

1. Defensive positions:

   1—pitcher

   2—catcher

   3—first base

   4—second base

   5—third base

   6—shortstop

   7—left field

   8—center field

   9—right field

2. Offensive performance:

   1B—one-base hit (single)

   2B—two base hit (double)

   3B—three-base hit (triple)

   HR—home run

   BB—base on balls (walk)

   KC—strike-out (called)

   KS—strikeout (swinging)

   E (pos.)—Error on defense (position number of player who made the error)

   FC—fielder's choice

   RBI—Runs batted in

   To record a putout, use the position numbers. Example: Tommy hit a ground ball to shortstop, who then caught the ball and threw to first base for the out. The correct scoring would be 6 (shortstop)–3 (first base.) If there is a double play, record the first out and then the second. Example: With a man on second. Tommy hit a ball to shortstop. Shortstop threw the ball to second for one out and the second baseman threw to first for the second out. The correct scoring would be 6–4–3. If the fielder makes the out unassisted, record the fielder's position number in the box.

   Note: Draw a line to the area that the ball was hit by the batter. Follow the runners around the baseline with a line, showing where they are at all times. You may lightly color in the diamond in the scorebook when a run scores.

3. Running symbols:

   SB—stolen base (catcher has the ball and runner advances)

   WP—pitcher throws a wild pitch past catcher and runner advances

   PB—catcher lets ball get passed him, runner advances

   B—balk

   E—error

   Use these symbols to describe why the runners advanced.

①	②	③	④	⑤	⑥ ⑦ ⑧ ⑨ ⑩ ⑪

NO.	PLAYER	P O S.	INN. / POS.	INN. / POS.	1	2	3
1	JOE SMITH	3			1 / Ks ◇ ①	◇	◇
3	MARK DOE	6			3 / BB ◇	◇	◇
10	BILL COLLINS	1	2	2	10 / 1B ◇	◇	◇
8	DAVID JONES	8			8 / 2B ① ◇	◇	◇
5	MIKE JOHNSON	2	2	1	5 / 6·3 ◇ ②	◇	◇
					R H E	R H E	R H E

⑫

1—Uniform number.
2—Name. There should be a slot for each player in the August League.
3—Position player is starting at. Not all players will have a starting position number.
4, 5—Inning and position substitution was made. Indicate if the substitution was made in the top of the inning or the bottom of the inning by placing a dot in the upper corner for the top of the inning or a dot in the bottom corner for the bottom of the inning.
6—Uniform number of player batting. This is not necessary in the August League since every player will be batting.
7—Number of outs.
8—Follow the players around diamond. Show where the ball was hit. Can lightly color in the diamond when a run scores.
9—Indicate what the batter does in this box.
10—Ball and strike counts. Follow the batter's count by checking off the appropriate box for each pitch.
11—RBIs. Place on top of the diamond and circle.
12—Runs, hits, and errors for each inning.

FIGURE 7-5

LITTLE LEAGUE BASEBALL QUIZ: RULES

	(Name)		
	Circle Correct Answer		
	True	or	*False*
1. Batter is out if he hits the ball with one foot outside the batter's box. [*6.03 and 6.06 (a)*]	T		F
2. Batter swings at third strike but is hit by the pitch, so goes to first. [*6.08 (b)*]	T		F
3. A batter can bunt on the third strike. [*6.05 (d)*]	T		F
4. A batter is out if he bunts down the first base line, running inside of it, and is hit by the thrown ball from the catcher to the first baseman. [*7.09 (k)*]	T		F
5. A substitute player must remain in the game until he has batted at least once and played at least six consecutive outs on defense. [*3.03*]	T		F
6. If two base runners end up on second base, . . . both runners are out. [*7.03*]	T		F
7. . . . second runner is automatically out. [*7.03*]	T		F
8. . . . second runner has to be tagged out. [*7.03*]	T		F
9. A base runner is out if hit by a batted ball before a fielder touched it. [*7.08 (f)*]	T		F
10. A base runner is out if hit by a batted ball after it touches a fielder's glove. [*7.09 (m)*]	T		F
11. A team may not pitch three 12-year-old boys in the same week. [*Reg. VI (c)*]	T		F
12. If a pitcher pitches four innings on Monday, he can still pitch two innings on Wednesday. [*Reg. VI (b)*]	T		F

13. According to the *infield fly rule*, the
    batter is automatically out if he hits
    an infield fly ball . . . with two outs
    and runners on first and second.   T   F
14. . . . with one out and runners on
    first and third.   T   F
15. . . . with no outs and the bases
    loaded.   T   F
16. . . . with one out and runners on
    first and second.   T   F
17. If both managers agree the field is
    playable, the umpire must start the
    game. [*3.10*]   T   F
18. Batter receives a walk and catcher
    immediately asks for time out but
    batter rounds first and goes to
    second base. Umpire should make
    batter return to first. [*5.10 (h)*]   T   F
19. First baseman, in fair territory,
    reaches across the foul line to catch
    a *foul fly*, but the ball bounces off
    his glove into fair territory. It is a
    fair ball.   T   F
20. Batted ball hits home plate and
    bounces in the air; catcher fields it
    in the air and throws runner out at
    first. Batter is out.   T   F
21. With a runner on base, it is a balk
    when the pitcher, without having the
    ball, stands on the pitching rubber.
    [*8.05*]   T   F
22. A runner leaves second base too
    soon and scores on the batter's
    single, and umpire sees the play. The
    runner must return to third. [*7.13*]   T   F
23. A runner may tag up and advance
    after a foul fly ball is caught.
    [*7.08 (d)*]   T   F
24. Runner on first steals second on a
    foul tip caught by the catcher.
    Runner must return to first.   T   F
25. Runner who runs more than three
    feet out of the base line to avoid
    interference with a fielder fielding a
    batted ball should be called out.
    [*7.08 (a)*]   T   F

26. Runners on first and third, one out;
    batter is automatically out when he
    hits an *infield fly*.   T   F
27. Catcher makes *tag* with back of
    gloved hand, which contains the
    ball, before the runner touches home
    plate. Runner is out.   T   F
28. Runner on first is hit by a batted
    ball while standing on the base.
    Runner is out. [*7.08 (f)*]   T   F
29. Runners on first and second, no
    outs. Batter hits infield fly which
    hits runner while standing on first.
    Runner is out. [*7.08 (f)*]   T   F
30. Batter bats out of turn and singles.
    With count 2 and 0 on next batter,
    appeal is made and first batter is
    called out. [*6.07*]   T   F
31. Runner on third leaves base too
    soon on a fly ball and scores.
    Umpire sees the infraction and
    should call the runner out. [*7.10 (a)*]   T   F

_____

Score

ANSWER KEY

1.	T	17.	T
2.	F	18.	F
3.	T	19.	F
4.	T	20.	T
5.	T	21.	T
6.	F	22.	F
7.	F	23.	T
8.	T	24.	F
9.	T	25.	F
10.	F	26.	F
11.	T	27.	T
12.	F	28.	T
13.	F	29.	F
14.	F	30.	F
15.	T	31.	F
16.	T		

8

STRATEGY FOR YOUR FUND-RAISING DRIVE

Many, Little League coaches have discovered the truth of the adage, "When you want a good job done, ask a busy person to do it." It is the fortunate manager or coach who doesn't find fund raising for his Little League team an expected part of his responsibility. I have coached in three leagues in three states, as my company transferred me around the country, and in only one of those leagues were the managers and coaches relieved of any fund-raising responsibilities.

That was a unique situation, the like of which I have not heard about in any other league. A group of businesspeople in the community, tired of constant harrassment throughout the year to give to this team or that team, the baseball program, or the youth football or basketball leagues, decided to concentrate their giving into one event per year. All teams and leagues agreed that there would be no direct solicitation of businesses at any other time during the year. It has become a sort of United Way approach to fundraising for youth sports in that town.

Tickets are sold to a fund-raising dinner. (Originally it was at $50 per plate, but it now has been increased to $100.) Of course, the cost of the meal (which is first class) and the raffle cash prizes have to be deducted from the gross proceeds, so only about 40 percent of the money "contributed" actually goes to the children's recreation programs. This is true, however, of just about any of the various types of fund-raising programs except pure solicitation. It might seem, therefore, that pure solicitation, including the jogathon and bikeathon, would be the most successful. However, that is not the case.

HELP FROM PROFESSIONALS

Fund raising has become a complex business, spawning companies of professional fund-raising consultants. They are skilled in the best ways to organize, conduct, and maximize results in a fund-raising campaign. Although it may appear that the *percentage* return on a dollar contributed is less when you use a professional, the net dollars earned will be more when you use a professional fund raiser. He will help you choose the best type of program for your group. If he spends much of his time in your area, he will know what fund-raising programs have been used, so you don't duplicate someone else's. He will have all the literature, forms, collection envelopes, and publicity material that are necessary in carrying out a successful campaign.

One of the most important elements that he will have is a prize program for the Little Leaguers who carry out the program. You would like to believe that just working for their Little League would be enough motivation for the kids who participate. Realistically, however, the most successful fund-raising campaigns are often those that offer the best prize program to motivate the youngsters.

Choosing the right products to sell is very important. For example, selling candy or other perishable foods represents serious problems in warm weather. Gift catalogs are the safest, in that regard, and have proved to be the best vehicle in my experience. No matter what time of year you conduct your campaign, there are gift-giving occasions that make gift catalogs appropriate. (How many mail order gift catalogs do you receive in the course of a year?)

The most successful fund-raising supplier I am familiar with is Bright of America, located in Summersville, West Virginia. If you inquire at your school, you can find out the name of the local distributor of Bright of America products. Or you can call them at (304) 872-3000.

Some professional fund-raising companies, specializing in youth fund raising, are as large as QSP, a division of *Reader's Digest*, with 300 full-time professional field sales managers. At the other extreme would be the independent fund raiser, who may be a one-person organization, working just in your area. These are the same companies that conduct fund-raising campaigns for school groups, so your local school would be a good place to go to find out who are the best fund-raising consultants serving in your area. Ask the principal, band director, PTA president, or any of the other sponsors of school fund-raising campaigns.

TIMING

The best timing for your fund-rasing campaign is to schedule it when it would conflict with the fewest other fund-raising drives in your community. The fall would be the worst time, because that is when most school fund-raising programs are conducted. Spring or summer would be the best time for two good reasons: There will be few if any other competing drives going on; and it is a time when professional fund-raising companies are least busy and therefore can devote more time and energy to your program.

Typically a professional fund consultant will ask you to organize a team of mothers to assist him, and they in turn will help motivate their children to do the selling. If you get a professional fund-raising consultant, who in turn works with the mothers and the kids, what does that leave for you to do? Coach your team!

9
STRATEGY FOR PLANNING A SUMMER INSTRUCTION LEAGUE

I have little fault to find with the way Little League, Inc. organizes the program nationally (actually, internationally), but one thing that has bothered me is the shortness of the season for the average Little Leaguer, particularly in the northern climates. If a league wishes to participate in the international All-Star competition, it must choose its players and start All-Star practice around July 1. To all intents, this ends the league's season, since it takes the key players from all teams and keeps them involved in All Star competition for the month of July and into August if they are not eliminated. In our league, which includes Little League and Senior League Baseball and Little League and Senior League Girls' Softball, we go from a program involving 500 children one week to a program involving only 70 children the next. The end of the season includes only All-Star team rosters of 14 players for Little League, 13-year-olds, and Senior League in baseball, and Little League and Senior League in softball. For the other 430 children, the season is over.

LITTLE LEAGUE CAMP

I sent my son Jim to Little League camp in Williamsport, Pennsylvania, for two summers (when he was 10 and 11), and I enthusiastically recommend that experience for any boys whose parents can do it. It isn't very expensive, and we car-pooled some boys from our league to Williamsport. Similar camps are offered by Little League, Inc., in Hillsgrove, Pennsylvania; St. Petersburg, Florida; Waco, Texas; and San Bernardino, California. The parent or coach who is interested should contact Little League headquarters in Williamsport at (717) 326-1921 for information on the nearest summer camp. The camps are conducted in two-week sessions during the summer and are always filled, so you are well advised to make your reservations early.

The camp provides baseball instruction in the morning and then two games per day, one in the afternoon and the other in the evening. Although there are some other activities, be assured that this is serious baseball, and a boy gets the equivalent of nearly another season of baseball with daily instruction for two weeks and about 20 games. Because the emphasis is on learning, some regular Little League rules are waived, such as allowing two games per day and allowing coaches to go out on the field and instruct players during the games.

INSTRUCTIONAL LEAGUE IN SUMMERSVILLE

Having seen how effective the summer instruction was with my son, but realizing that few boys would have the opportunity to go to an official Little League baseball camp, we decided to organize an instructional league in our community.

An instructional league may be operated by any Little League program, but whether your Little League insurance covers your program may depend on when it is in operation. Call Mr. Daniel Kirby of Little League headquarters in Williamsport, Pennsylvania, to clarify your program and to be sure insurance coverage will be in effect.

Our league hired a high school coach to direct our two-week camp, but our league organized the curriculum. Some of our coaches, who could plan around their respective work schedules, assisted.

We planned the camp for boys from 8 through 11 (current league age). We excluded boys who were league age 12, since they would be playing Senior League the next year, but included 8-year-olds, since they would be league age 9 the next year, and eligible to play Little League ball.

Essentially we followed the Williamsport Little League daily schedule:

9:00 A.M.–noon	Instruction
Noon–1:00 P.M.	Lunch
1:00 P.M.–3:00 P.M.	First games
3:00 P.M.–4:00 P.M.	Swim
6:00 P.M.–7:30 P.M.	Second games
7:30 P.M.–9:00 P.M.	Second games

The parents dropped off their boys at 9:00 A.M., picked them up again at 4:00 P.M., and returned them for the evening game. The boys brought their lunch, and we provided the drinks.

The camp was organized into teams, and T-shirts and caps were provided. We had the use of three fields, one lighted, so we could have three afternoon games simultaneously, two in the early evening, and one under the lights at night. Fortunately, there was a county swimming pool in the same recreational complex as our fields, and we made arrangements for our campers to swim there.

We charged the campers $10, but our league treasury had to underwrite part of the cost. Our refreshment stand was open in the evening, and the profit from it helped to defray some of the costs. We obtained coaches and umpires from adult volunteers, augmented by high school students, whom we paid a stipend.

With three fields at our disposal, we could teach the basics of hitting on one field (with a pitching machine), defense (infield and outfield) on another field, and pitching and catching on a third field, and rotate the players from one field to another (see Figures 9-1, 9-2, and 9-3).

9-1. Boys take turns learning second-base position.

9-2. Second baseman touches base on force play.

9-3. Getting rid of ball quickly and accurately is drilled to infielders.

INSTRUCTIONAL LEAGUE IN ST. MATTHEWS

I thought we had designed something unique with a summer instructional camp, but found out in talking with Mike Powers that his league in St. Matthews, Kentucky, had also done something similar, with some interesting differences.

Instead of confining the camp to two weeks, all day, as we did, they ran it for the month of August (after most All-Star teams are finished) and conducted it in the evenings as a summer league, with each team playing two games per week. They also had two leagues, one for 7- and 8-year-olds, and one for boys 9, 10, and 11. Figure 9–4 is the information sheet for the St. Matthews Instructional League, and Figure 9–5 is the application form. The special game rules that were used in the St. Matthews Instructional League were as follows:

FIGURE 9-4

St. Matthews August Instructional League Information Sheet

WHAT: St. Matthews August Instructional League

WHO: Any 7–11-year-old playing this year

TIME: Season opens July 28, and ends August 30
10-game schedule, 2 games per week—
weeknights only

COST: $15.00 per player

UNIFORMS: Cap and T-shirt included in cost

REASON: Improve fundamental skills, especially
batting

LEAGUES: 7–8-year-olds: pitching machine pitch/no
steals or walks

9–11-year-olds: modified minor league rules

BRIEF SUMMARY OF MODIFIED INSTRUCTIONAL LEAGUE RULES

Both Leagues
1. Six innings or 1½ hours, whichever comes first
2. No pick-up players allowed
3. Round-robin batting order
4. Minimum play: six outs on defense
5. Unlimited substitutions, except pitcher

9, 10 & 11 League
Regular Little League pitching rules, except: no player
shall pitch more than 3 innings per game

If you have not been assigned to a team by July 16 or if you
have any questions, ask or call:

Barbara Shaffer   Margaret Streck
555-1708—W   555-8207—H
555-4212—H

FIGURE 9-5

St. Matthews August Instructional League Application
PLEASE READ CAREFULLY
* * INSTRUCTIONS * *

1. Fill in all information on this form. You will be called to supply missing data. Your application will not be processed until all information is available.
2. Enclose payment with application, place in envelope, seal, <u>print</u> name and age of child on envelope and return to concession stand. Please pay by check—THERE WILL BE NO CASH RECEIPTS ISSUED. Sign-up deadline is *Saturday, June 21.*

PLEASE PRINT

Child's Name_____ Birthdate_____

Parent's Name_____ Spouse_____

Address_____ Phone_____

Group Health Insurance Plan and Number_____

1. Did you play in St. Matthews Little League this year?_____
   If so, what team?_____

2. If you played in another league:
   What league?_____
   Name/phone of coach_____

3. Do you anticipate any extended absence during the summer season (vacation, camp, etc.)? If so, when?_____

4. For carpool purposes, *if possible*, place applicant on team with:

5. St. Matthews Little League runs on *volunteer* manpower. Will you help as ☐ Manager ☐ Coach ☐ Scorekeeper ☐ Other_____

_____
Signature of Parent or Guardian

Little League Games

1. Use Little League Rules except as modified herein.
2. Unlimited substitution.
3. Bat the roster. (All substitutes bat in order prior to the lead-off batter hitting a second time, regardless of whether or not the substitute plays defensively.)
4. Pitcher is limited to a maximum three innings in any given game except once during the season when a team is scheduled to play on successive nights. Then, and only then, one pitcher may pitch six innings in one of the two games so scheduled.
5. No forfeits or rescheduling of rained-out games.
6. If one team has an insufficient number of players to field nine, said team may use a substitute from the opponent's roster.
7. Minor League 10-Run Rule (regular season) will apply— no team can score more than 10 runs in a half inning under any circumstances. When the 10th run is scored, the half inning is concluded regardless of number of outs, and the next half inning commences.
8. Length of the game is the same as the Minor League (regular season)—6 innings or 1½ hours of play, whichever comes first. This includes ties, since no won-lost records are kept.

Minor League Games

1. Use Little League Rules except as modified herein.
2. Unlimited substitution.
3. Bat the roster.
4. Pitches will be delivered to the batter by the pitching machine operated and adjusted by the manager or coach of the offensive team.
5. There will be no walks or called strikes. However, once a batter has two strikes (swinging), the batter must swing at one of the next two pitches. If the batter hits a foul ball on said swing, the requirement of swinging at one of the next two pitches starts again. The penalty for failure to swing at one of the two pitches is a called strikeout.

6. Runners may not advance on catcher's return throws to the mound.

7. If a batted ball hits the pitching machine or the adult feeding the machine prior to touching a defensive player, the ball is declared dead, no advance by runners can occur, and the play is nullified. The batter returns to the plate and resumes his turn at bat.

8. If a ball thrown by the defense hits the pitching machine, it is a live ball and play continues.

9. No forfeits or rescheduling of rained-out games.

10. If one team has an insufficient number of players to field nine, said team may use a substitute from the opponent's roster.

11. Minor League 10-Run rules (regular season) will apply—no team can score more than 10 runs in a half inning under any circumstances. When the 10th run is scored, the half inning is concluded regardless of outs, and the next half inning commences.

12. Length of the game is the same as the Minor League (regular season)—6 innings or 1½ hours of play, whichever comes first. No inning can begin after 1½ hours have elapsed. This includes ties, since no won-lost records are kept.

13. Adult coaches may be used. (Note—Minor League only.)

14. The assigned umpire will be the umpire in charge and will exercise all decisions relative to rule interpretations. In addition, he will make all judgment calls on fly balls, call all bases except home plate, and keep account of the number of strikes on the batter. The assigned umpire will determine if the batter did swing and observe runners for leaving the base too soon.

15. In addition to the assigned umpire, one adult will be selected from the stands to assist. This assistance is limited to determining if a batted ball is fair (point) or foul (shout "Foul Ball") and exercising judgment on safe/out calls at home plate only. It will not be necessary for this adult to wear the protective gear, since he will not be behind the catcher as the pitch is delivered.

FIGURE 9-6

Department of Athletics

University of Louisville
Louisville, Kentucky 40292
(502) 588-5732

UNIVERSITY of LOUISVILLE

PLAYER _Tom Powers_

1986
CARDINAL BASEBALL CAMP
EVALUATION

HITTING

STRENGTHS	WEAKNESSES
____ Knuckles aligned *not aligned*	____ Hands apart
✓ Good starting position	____ Too low
✓ Top hand over	____ Hitches (props hands)
✓ Hands on bat to follow thru	____ Uppercut swing
✓ Good arm extension	____ No arm extension
✓ Smooth follow thru	____ Stops arms during swing
____ Good arm strength	____ Cannot handle bat
____ Bat in proper position	✓ Stiff front arm
✓ Eyes level to pitcher	____ Eyes slanted to pitcher
✓ Head stays on ball thru swing	____ Pulls head away from ball
____ Level shoulders	✓ Front shoulder too high
____ Front shoulder to ball	✓ Front shoulder pulls off ball
✓ Hips level thru swing	____ Hips locked
____ Hips open during swing	____ Hips do not point to ball
✓ Comfortable distance apart	____ Stance too narrow
✓ Good balance	____ Improper balance
____ Front foot open	✓ Closed front foot
✓ Good stride distance	____ Stride is too long
✓ Foot strides forward	____ Steps in bucket
	✓ Back foot moves

COMMENTS: _Radar gun speed 56_
Good tools. With good coaching could be an excellent pitcher.

Academic and Athletic Excellence

Mike Powers advocates a personal evaluation of each
player at the end of the instructional league for both his use
and the use of his coach next year. He uses an evaluation
form to score the strengths and weaknesses of a player in the
areas of hitting, pitching, and fielding. Mike's son Tom went
to the Cardinal Baseball Camp, sponsored by the University
of Louisville, and Mike uses similar evaluation forms to those

FIGURE 9-7

Department of Athletics

University of Louisville
Louisville, Kentucky 40292
(502) 588-6732

UNIVERSITY of LOUISVILLE

PLAYER_____

1986
CARDINAL BASEBALL CAMP
EVALUATION

PITCHING

STRENGTHS

- ✓ Eyes remain on target
- ✓ Good rock step
- ✓ Good pivot on rubber
- ✓ Closes hips
- ✓ Good balance point
- ✓ Good lower body thrust
- ✓ 360 arm extension
- ✓ Good follow thru
- Front foot across mid-line
- Front foot on ball of foot
- ✓ Good fielding position

WEAKNESSES

- Does not pick up target
- Poor rock step
- Poor pivot on rubber
- Hips open
- Poor balance point
- Needs to use lower body
- ✓ Short arms (less extension)
- Does not follow thru
- Throws across body
- ✓ Front foot lands on heel
- Poor fielding position

COMMENTS:

FIELDING (Infield)

STRENGTHS

- ✓ Balanced starting position
- ✓ Weight on balls of feet
- Rear end down
- Arms extended when fielding
- ✓ Fields ball in front
- ✓ Steps toward direction of throw
- ✓ Arm extended
- ✓ Good follow thru

WEAKNESSES

- Stance too wide
- Off balance at start
- ✓ Brings rear end up
- ✓ Fields too close to body
- Fields off to the side
- Throws across body
- Short arm
- ✓ Does not complete arm rotation

COMMENTS: When pitching, try not to break your hands before your windup. The opposing hitter will be able to see what pitch is coming.

Academic and Athletic Excellence

developed by that camp. In Figures 9–6 and 9–7, Mike shares his son Tom's evaluation with us.

Each league will have its own strengths and limitations for the conducting of a summer instructional league in terms of facilities and personnel. Be assured of one thing, however: you will have plenty of kids ready, willing, and eager to participate.

10
STRATEGY FOR WINNING

Up to this point, you haven't read much about winning, but if it weren't important, why would we keep score? Keeping winning in proper perspective is a problem, however, especially with parents and coaches. Ironically, the boys, who do the winning or losing, are the least concerned so long as they are having fun.

Let's face it; it is more fun for everyone concerned when your team wins, but there are different degrees of winning. To me, a team has had a winning season if it has won more games than it lost. Some parents and coaches aren't satisfied unless their team wins *every* game, or at least the league championship. Unfortunately, that attitude toward winning puts the kind of pressure on winning that takes the fun out of playing.

I can give you a formula for a winning season: winning more games than you lose. It is a simple formula based on time spent. The more time you and your team spend, the more games you will win. If you spend more time coaching and your team spends more time practicing than any other team in the league, chances are you will win the most games in the league. That is why the Taiwanese All-Star Team has dominated the Little League World Series over the years. Chinese boys are not bigger and stronger than American boys; if anything, it is the opposite. But as the manager of the championship Taiwan team pointed out, their boys are *disciplined to learn from repetition*, starting with their education, and continuing into their sports. They practice, practice, practice! And when the basics of baseball have been practiced enough, they become routine in a game.

PRACTICING

At the 1986 Little League World Series, Steve Keener, a Little League executive, commented on the differences between the Taiwanese and the American boys before the World Series in Williamsport. The Chinese boys were always practicing baseball, whereas the American boys were taking time out to go swimming, play horseshoes, and so on. Both were interested in winning, so it was just a matter of degree.

In our league of 10 teams, there were noticeable differences in the approach of teams preparing for a winning season. At one extreme, a group of parents petitioned the league to have the manager removed because he held only three practices the entire previous season. Our team was probably at the other extreme; we practiced nearly every day we did not have a game. Did we win the league championship? No, we won the second half of the season, but lost in the championship game to the team that won the first half, a team that practiced just about as much as we did. But we had a winning season (a 13–5 record), the 20th consecutive winning season in my coaching experience! That's why I can share the secrets of how to win. The first is to put in the necessary time, because there is a cause/effect relationship.

Our team practices nearly every day we don't have a game. The kids love it, if you make practice fun, as we have tried to promote in this book. When they go into higher levels of school athletics, they will certainly practice every day, so their parents may as well get used to it, if they want their children to have the enjoyment of participating in sports. Can you be there every day to direct the practice? Probably not, if you have work and family schedules that come first, so you will have to spend the time on the next secret to a winning season: choosing your coaches.

CHOOSING YOUR COACHES

I have never had fewer than three coaches assisting me, and have had as many as five. Usually they are fathers of team members, but occasionally there are older brothers, and in some rare cases men not related to the players. It is important in considering coaches that you find out their background in playing and/or coaching baseball. A willing father with no playing or coaching background can still help you in some capacity, but you don't want to embarrass him by asking him to do something he is incapable of doing. (I learned that the hard way by asking a dad to hit fly balls to a group of outfielders, but he was so uncoordinated that he just couldn't make contact between the ball and the bat, let alone hit fly balls!)

If you know of dads who were good Minor League managers, whose sons are ready for Little League, you could get a big bonus in drafting their sons by getting the dads as coaches, as well. Do you take the risk of getting a redneck parent as a coach? Possibly, but not if your league has done a good job of promoting and enforcing the proper Little League philosophy throughout your organization, including your Minor League. I have had several redneck fathers as coaches and have had the satisfaction of converting them in the course of the season. With three or more coaches, you can schedule practice every day and be sure at least two adults will be there.

SCOUTING

The next secret of having a winning season is scouting. Part of your time as a manager and coach must be spent in scouting for next year's players and coaches. If you can't actually watch some Minor League games, you should at least call the managers of the Minor League teams whose players you can draft the next year, and get a line on who their best players are. Do it *this* year, however, because if you wait until next spring, their memories will be less accurate.

Scout the midget football and basketball leagues in the fall and winter to see who the best athletes are. Sometimes good athletes will move in during the summer who would not have been in your Little League organization the previous spring. Occasionally you will spot that big, aggressive natural athlete who you know will excel in any sport.

I also use the kids returning to my team as scouts, but mostly as "negative screeners." They can tell you which players are least likely to succeed, but sometimes tout the others more on the basis of friendship than ability.

Thorough scouting takes time, but that's what will make the difference between winning and losing: the time you put into it! If you have done your scouting homework well, you should go to your player draft meeting with the boys you want, ranked in order of choice. I have prided myself over the years in being able to pick out future All-Stars, whether our team drafted them or another team, with a high degree of predictability.

CHARTING

Charting is the paperwork of coaching that many coaches and managers just won't take the time to do. It is another test of how much time a manager is willing to devote to producing a winning team. The charts I would recommend are:

- Time Chart
- Pitching Chart
- Fielding Chart
- Batting Chart

The Time Chart is designed to record three significant running times for each boy:

- the time to run from home to first
- the time to steal second
- the time to circle the bases

10-1. Keep track of how many pitches your pitchers throw. A young arm can tire easily.

They are simple time tests, run periodically with a stopwatch, to keep a record of the relative speed of your players. In a crucial game where you would like a runner to steal second to put him in a scoring position, it helps to know how fast that boy on first is.

The Pitching Chart is designed to record the following statistics each time a boy pitches (whether in practice, a practice game, or a real game):

- balls
- low strikes
- high strikes
- walks
- strikeouts
- hits
- runs
- batters hit
- batters faced
- total number of pitches (see Figure 10-1)

The Fielding Chart is for keeping a running record on the defensive play of your team. It can be taken from the official scorebook after each game, provided you have taught your scorekeeper how to keep the score accurately. It should record for each player:

- ground ball assists
- infield putouts
- pop-ups caught
- fly balls caught
- line drives caught
- ground ball errors
- pop-up errors
- fly ball errors
- thrown ball errors
- attempted catching errors
- passed balls (catcher)

The Batting Chart (Figure 10–2) is the typical batting average analysis used in major-league baseball. One important statistic I use is total times on base (TOB). It may be the most significant statistic of all in Little League, because a much higher percentage of runs is scored once a player gets on base (whether by walk, error, or hit) in Little League, compared to higher levels of baseball. Consequently, I look carefully at a player's TOB percentage. If it is good, it shows me that the player knows how to work a pitcher to get on base; he is patient enough to work him for a walk, and he is savvy enough to know when to expect a "fat" pitch to hit. Usually a boy with a good on-base average also strikes out rarely, and is a good prospect for the leadoff batter. You will note that is true of the top two boys in TOB in Figure 10–2. As a matter of fact, your lineup, after a few games, should be dictated by the performance of your players as measured by the Batting Chart.

Keeping statistics has been helpful to me as manager of the All-Star Team, because I used them in deciding who my starters should be. In every practice for the two weeks before

FIGURE 10-2

GIANT AVERAGES, FIRST HALF (9 GAMES)

PLAYER	G	TAB	W	HP	S	OAB	H	TOB	R	2B	3B	HR	RBI	SO	BATT. AVG.
Lane Acree	7	14	0	0	0	14	6	6	4	0	2	0	2	5	.429
Jim Beirne	9	33	5	0	0	28	10	15	11	0	3	0	8	5	.357
Rod Blankenship	8	19	2	0	0	17	6	8	6	1	0	0	5	4	.353
Rodney Cox	9	13	3	1	0	9	2	6	0	0	0	0	0	6	.222
Jeff Girod	9	13	1	1	0	11	5	7	2	2	0	0	0	2	.455
Mike Grose	7	9	1	0	0	8	3	4	3	1	0	0	2	1	.375
John Hoard	9	20	4	0	0	16	6	10	3	1	0	0	0	3	.375
David Joo	9	25	4	0	0	21	11	15	8	0	2	0	7	4	.524
Mike Lipscomb	9	17	2	1	0	14	5	8	3	0	1	0	3	8	.357
Jim McIntosh	9	34	6	0	1	27	15	21	12	1	0	0	6	4	.556
Mark Proctor	9	35	5	0	1	29	17	22	13	2	0	1	9	0	.586
Chuck Thomas	9	16	1	0	0	15	7	8	3	0	0	0	6	2	.467
Mike Walton	9	17	3	1	0	13	2	5	3	0	0	0	0	10	.154
Paul Williams	9	30	5	0	0	25	12	17	9	5	2	1	13	6	.480

KEY: G (Games); TAB (Total times at bat); W (Walk); HP (Hit by pitched ball); S (Sacrifice); OAB (official times at bat); H (Hits); TOB (Total times on base); R (Runs scored); 2B (Doubles); 3B (Triples); HR (Home runs); RBI (Runs batted in); SO (Strike outs); Batt. Avg. (Batting Average -- number of hits divided by official times at bat).

our first All-Star game, I had a practice game as the last part of each practice session. I told the players that they would be charted and that the lineup would be dictated by how they did cumulatively.

Unfortunately, the son of one of my coaches did poorly in the practice games, so didn't start. It could have been a touchy situation, except that I had announced my plans in the beginning and everyone understood what they were. Ironically, the coach's son didn't play until the late innings of the second game, but hit a home run his first time at bat. It was a case where desire overcame the statistics!

PITCHING ROTATION

In our league two games per week are scheduled for each team. This has created an ongoing debate among coaches on whether it is better to pitch your two best pitchers six innings each or have them go three and three in both games. To me, it is a question that has no pat answer. I will sometimes start a pitcher with the intention of pitching him only three innings, but then he will have such an easy time in the first three innings, with good control, that it would be a mistake to take him out just to save him for the next game.

The biggest mistake Little League managers make with their pitching strategy is looking ahead to the next game, instead of concentrating on winning the present game.

On the other hand, if you are charting your pitchers, you need to watch the number of pitches a player makes as one indication of how he is doing. If he gets behind on every batter, gives a lot of walks and hits, and your defense is committing a lot of errors, that pitcher in three innings may be throwing more pitches than he did in a previous six-inning game. You often hear TV and radio play-by-play announcers comment on how many pitches a pitcher has thrown. Why do you think they consider it a significant statistic? When was the last time you kept track of that statistic on your pitchers?

Another mistake many Little League managers make is keeping a pitcher in the game too long when he isn't being effective. This is another case where your statistics can help you, if you can ask the coach who is doing the chart how many pitches the pitcher has thrown, how many low strikes, and how many walks.

Yanking a pitcher can be more traumatic to a child (and his parents) in Little League than in higher levels of baseball, but there is a gentle way to do it. I usually warn my pitcher first that I may have to replace him, and when I do replace him, it usually involves the pitcher taking another position, rather than taking a downhearted walk to the dugout. Ironically he rarely disagrees with you about changing pitchers; he is the one most acutely aware that he doesn't have it, and you can help his morale by reminding him that all pitchers are like that: "Some days they have it, and other days they don't."

The decision about taking a pitcher out is dictated in part by who you have left to put in. As I mentioned in the chapter on pitching, you need four players capable of pitching. Any fewer, and you may find yourself in the situation I described where we had to play three games in a week, the third, a postponed game, back to back with the second game. Our best pitcher pitched six innings in the first game, our second pitcher pitched six innings in the second game, which went into extra innings. So we also had to pitch our third pitcher in the second game, which made him ineligible to pitch in the third game the next day.

Three pitchers are too few, and five or more are too many, so four pitchers is the right number. To have more will mean that you will not be giving some of them enough work to keep in good pitching shape.

In terms of pitching strategy, I mentioned in the pitching chapter that your pitcher should concentrate on throwing low strikes to the top four or five batters in the opposing lineup, with an occasional change-up or curve ball when he is ahead on the count. The four or five boys in the lower end of the lineup, he should just challenge with his fastball. He can even pitch to them from the stretch position, which will reduce his speed but improve his control. The last thing you want him to do is give a walk to a weak hitter.

A pitcher's concentration on pitching may be so intense (as it should be) that he will forget his fielding responsibility when the time comes. That is where you must do your part as a coach in reminding him from the bench, or in a coach/ pitcher conference. For example, with a runner on third I always remind my pitcher he must cover home if the ball gets through the catcher; in a bunting situation, I remind my pitcher (as well as my other infielders) to watch for a bunt. Incidentally, I study the other manager's signals and try to pick up the bunt sign. It is always amusing when you can do that and call out to your infield, "Watch for the bunt," just after the manager has flashed the bunt sign to his batter. The look on the batter's face of "Now what do I do?" is always priceless!

A great morale booster for a pitcher after a strikeout (when the bases are empty) is to have the catcher fire that ball to the third baseman, and as the infield folds in toward the pitcher's mound, the ball is tossed from third baseman to second baseman to shortstop, back to the third baseman, who hands the ball to the pitcher. His teammates, at the mound, give the pitcher encouragement and it not only boosts his confidence, but puts a little extra apprehension in the mind of the next batter, witnessing that burst of enthusiasm. The exercise is diagrammed in Chart 10, and should be drilled in practice.

BATTING STRATEGY

The first four positions in your batting order should be filled with your best hitters for the obvious reason that they will get more times at bat. Your leadoff batter should be a player who has a high TOB percentage. As mentioned earlier, he will rarely strike out, which means that he will either walk or make contact with the ball, which will get him on base via either hit or error.

The second batter in the lineup may be your best bunter, and should also have a high TOB percentage. The third batter in the lineup should be your best hitter, and your fourth-place batter your best slugger. (Sometimes your best hitter in

CHART 10. AFTER-STRIKEOUT DRILL
(with no one on base)

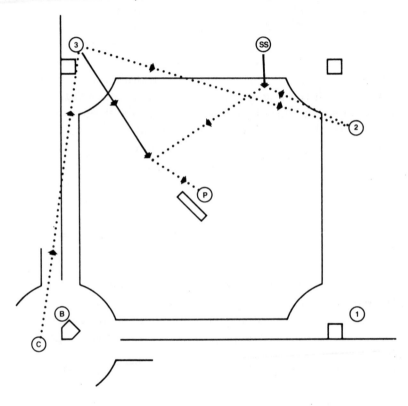

Key:

•••••••••• Path of thrown ball

———— Path of infielder

Moving toward pitcher

batting average will be a singles hitter, whereas your best slugger will be an extra-base hitter—when he connects.) I rarely substitute in the first four or five places in the lineup, knowing that the combination of my best hitters, back-to-back, will come up to bat at least three times during the game.

I always consider it a bonus when one of the batters in the lower half of the lineup gets on base, so I will probably plan the strategy of coaxing a walk with them more so than with the good hitters on the team. Consequently I will give the take sign more often on a 2-and-0, or 3-and-1 count, and will *always* give it on a 3-and-0 count, to a boy in the lower half of the batting order. Statistically we have found that 2 out of 3 walks will result in a run, so I play for the averages and try to get our weak hitters on base any way we can.

I don't use the major-league strategy of having a batter bunt on the first pitch if there is a runner on first with fewer than two outs. Because there are so many wild pitches and passed balls in Little League, it is the exception when a runner on first doesn't get an easy steal to second. However, to help create a wild pitch or passed ball, I will frequently give the batter the fake-bunt sign, telling him to lean over the plate and only pull back at the last moment, in order to distract both pitcher and catcher. That will often get your runner to second base without sacrificing the batter. Even if it doesn't work, it will have the infield coming in on the next pitch, expecting a bunt, while you have given the hit sign to the batter. If he makes contact with the ball, it will probably go through for a hit.

BASE-RUNNING STRATEGY

I mentioned the strategy of run when you walk in the chapter on base running, but sometimes your batters have to be reminded when the time comes. A code word, like "Tiger!" will remind them without tipping off the opposition. I have seen the strategy of taking an extra base work with some

10-3. You have to remind runners to run on a ground ball to avoid the force-out.

teams nearly every time, particularly if they are not strong up the middle defensively, and are caught off guard by the play.

Constant reminders from the dugout to your base runners and base coaches are necessary. Before every pitch is not too often to point out the situation:

- "No outs—don't take chances."
- "Two outs—run on anything."
- "You're forced on a ground ball" (see Figure 10–3).
- "Tag up on a fly."

One of the most critical base-running plays that requires coaching comes up when a runner is on third. If a wild pitch or passed ball occurs, the runner has to decide whether to attempt to steal home. As coach, you must have done your part in analyzing the following:

- Does the pitcher cover home?
- Does the catcher toss his helmet, or try to see the play through the face guard?
- Is the catcher a rookie or experienced?
- Is the pitcher a rookie or experienced?
- Is the runner on third fast?

You have to evaluate the situation and then let your runner know what to do ahead of time. Trying to coach him *when* the situation occurs is almost impossible, since he will be hearing all kinds of advice from parents and teammates at the same time.

We will try our situation play called zebra with a runner on third base if some of these conditions are present:

- Our base runner is fast.
- There are two outs and a weak hitter at bat.
- The third baseman and/or catcher are rookies.

The idea of the play is for the base runner to deliberately draw a throw from the pitcher or catcher and force a rundown between third and home. The situation in which it is most likely to succeed is when the third baseman plays off the bag, which gives the runner the chance to go three or four steps down the line after each pitch (see Figure 10-4). The runner should make a break for the plate the instant the catcher throws the ball to either the pitcher or the third baseman, because while the runner is running and sliding into home, the ball has to be thrown and caught twice, from the catcher and then back to the catcher. That means five chances of an error: two throwing, two catching, and one tagging. If I have a fast runner with a three- or four-step lead, I'll take my chances!

MOTIVATIONAL STRATEGY

Managing kids can be so frustrating sometimes, but so rewarding most of the time. At the Little League age, they are

10-4. When third baseman plays way off the bag, the base runner can move far down the line after the pitch crosses the plate—an ideal situation for "zebra" play.

so trusting and so impressionable that it places a heavy responsibility on the adult who is their leader to justify their trust and impress them in a positive way.

Keeping things in perspective is the coach's biggest challenge. The pressure to win makes it very difficult for him to empathize with the player who just blew it and lost the game. But empathize he must! A pat on the back or a reassuring word, instead of a dirty look or a chewing out, can go a long way toward defusing the pressure and sense of failure the "goat" is feeling.

Getting the coach's approval is important to a kid, and the sensitive coach will soon recognize how great a motivator encouragement is. But he also has to recognize that levels of accomplishment vary greatly among the boys on his team. What is a routine play for an All-Star is a milestone for a rookie.

In *Managing Little League Baseball*, I mentioned what a great motivator the "Stargell Stars" were with my team. Willie Stargell, when he was team captain of the world-champion Pittsburgh Pirates in the late seventies, gave gold-plated stars to his teammates when they made exceptional plays, and they pinned them on their caps. Our Little League team colors are black and orange, so we bought some inexpensive orange felt stars, which contrasted nicely with our black caps.

The players were awarded their stars after each game, based on exceptional performance at each child's level of ability. All rookies got a star when they got their first hit and their first putout in the field. Last season one boy who was still looking for his first star at midseason was the only player to help the coaches clean out the dugout after a game, and we gave him a star for that. (We had lots of help after that.)

The point was that any player who did something special *for him* to help the team got a star. The kids lined up after each game—win or lose—as if we were giving out $10 gold pieces, instead of felt stars that only cost us two cents!

That symbol of coach recognition and approval meant that much to a player. And he made sure it was sewn on his cap before the next game.

In *Managing Little League Baseball*, I reported that we had to abandon our stars because one of the other managers cited Rule 1, 11, which says all uniforms must be identical. Technically he was correct, but the next year I made a good enough case before our league board of directors that the "Stargell Stars" were a positive motivator that they allowed it, on an optional basis, as a local league rule.

In a way, the "Stargell Star," which recognizes a player's contribution to his team at his ability level, is the exact opposite of the winning-is-everything philosophy in sports that unfortunately creeps into Little League baseball sometimes.

As a manager or coach, you will have a winning season if you put in the necessary time and your players practice, practice, practice. And you personally will be a winner in the eyes of your kids if they remember you as a coach who always recognized their triumphs and empathized with their defeats. Long after they have forgotten the scores of the games, they will still remember the coach who cared about them.

INDEX